Rideshare Cowboy:

My Ministry on Wheels

By Thomas L. Beshears

2

Table of Contents

Prologue

Chapter 1: Memories

Chapter 2: Work

Chapter 3: Love

Chapter 4: Sin

Chapter 5: Hope

Chapter 6: Joy

Chapter 7: The King's Highway

Acknowledgments

About the Author

4

To the Lord God Almighty (Our Father) and my beautiful wife Rose

Prologue

My first ride of the night began at a local psych ward.

As a rideshare driver, I enjoy some flexibility. I accept the rides I choose to accept and decline those I prefer not to take through the ride share app of the company I drive for. Overall, in my eight years of driving, I have accepted and completed well over 90 percent of the rides offered me through the app.

In the spring of 2022, I accepted a ride offering leading me from the outer Dallas area east of the city towards Richardson, a city among an inner ring of suburbs. Accepting the opportunity I steered "Old Red" (my red 2007 Toyota Camry) onto the President George Bush Turnpike and headed west.

The George Bush is a critical and well-known part of the transportation network for the Dallas-Fort Worth area. Forming a semicircle around much of DFW, the turnpike looks on the map like a jagged hook running from northeast to southwest, girding part of what we call the Metroplex. As Texas has produced two Presidents George Bush, it's unclear to me which president is being honored (I suspect most Texans are just as uncertain). Along with local freeways named after President Lyndon Johnson and former Speakers of the House Sam Rayburn and

Jim Wright, the names are mostly a reminder of how many important politicians the Lone Star State has sent to Washington over the years.

This night, one of these highways would lead me to the psych ward, and James. Know that this is not his real name; I use pseudonyms for my passengers in this book to protect their privacy. James was waiting outside the emergency room at a hospital off Campbell in Richardson. As is the case when I pick up a new rider, I really had no idea what to expect. When I am called to a hospital, the people requesting a ride can be almost anyone: administrators, doctors, nurses, an employee going home, a patient being released from care, a relative who has left the side of a loved one, or simply a visitor. The gentleman who hailed me this night was clearly of the first category. He was getting off work.

James was a Black man, middle-aged, around six feet. He was heavy-set, with short hair. Wearing blue scrubs, he carried a professional black leather bag containing his effects for the day's work. I picked him up around 5 p.m. The rideshare app told me James was going to the eastern exurbs of Dallas, near Lake Ray Hubbard.

The ride began, as many do, with small talk about the weather. It is a harmless subject we all care about, a light topic that brings strangers together.

"That storm that just blew through is the first bad weather we've had in a while," I said, referring to a thunderstorm overnight that had put a dent in our north Texas drought.

"Sure was," he replied.

"Looks like you're getting off work," I said.

"Just ended my shift."

James indicated he was a counselor at the facility. Then something about the way he discussed his work, and his patients, indicated he was, shall we say, spiritually inclined. It became clear he was a believer, a servant of Christ. This was remarkable because he worked in an industry that often marginalizes Christians.

My policy is to try to meet people where they're at. When he made clear he was open to "spiritual things," I welcomed the opportunity.

"I am a believer in prayer," James said.

"So am I, brother," I responded, full of joy.

As I drove him home, he shared how difficult it is to work amidst the chaos of the day. "Many people are having emotional and mental problems," James noted. "I see it every day. It's getting worse."

"What do you think is the real problem driving it?" I asked.

"They don't know God. They don't know prayer. They don't know Jesus."

"Amen," I said.

He shared more about the kind of patients coming in, the growing numbers of people afflicted with anxiety, depression and addictions. I tried to encourage him in his work.

And so it went. We shared our hearts with one another, growing closer to the Lord and sharing in His Presence. I could tell he was disappointed he couldn't share more of his faith with his patients. Fortunately, I don't have the same limitations on me as a rideshare driver, though I can't speak with complete freedom while in someone else's employ.

When I dropped off James at his home, I felt I had gained a friend. And I think both of us took something from the conversation.

James picked up a little encouragement and support from a stranger who admired what he was doing day in and day out. I was inspired by his commitment to sharing Jesus Christ in a profession of psychology that has practically evicted all faith from diagnosis and treatment.

It was clear he knew he was limited in the tools he could use to try to help people in his job. And it was clear James saw he was selling his patients short because of these limits placed on him and his work. He recognized psychology wasn't the answer for the crowds of people seeking treatment for devastated lives and souls. The answer, of course, is, was and eternally will be our Lord and Savior Jesus Christ.

After we parted that night, I believe both of us gave glory to God for the experience. I certainly did.

From my years of living abroad, I have become fluent in German. I have studied the Holy Scriptures using multiple versions in both English and German. From this I have grown in my understanding of His Holy Word. Years ago my attention was drawn to Romans 1:8-12 and a deeper understanding of these verses in both languages. I am impressed and inspired at how a humble Apostle Paul expressed his longing to visit the brethren in Rome and impart some spiritual gift to them that they may be more established. Moreover, he wished to experience the exchange (German: *Wechselwirkung*, or "exchanging effect") or interaction of sharing each other's faith (*Gnadengabe*, or "Grace Gifts"). It is my hope to experience the same interaction (*Wechselwirkung*) in a much smaller way wherever life takes me. As I see it, my job is to be present in the moment for Jesus—doing His work right here, right now no matter what comes my way.

While sharing my ride and my time with people such as James, unique individuals who have tough jobs in which they're spiritually hamstrung by their profession, I remember how each conversation can, through the person or persons hearing it, ultimately touch countless lives.

While this was not a ride in which I directed somebody to Jesus, the time I spent with James— and now share with you—is an important example of how these rides are an opportunity for fellowship as well as the winning or fortification (*Befestigung*) of souls. Something being overlooked in the "new economy" is that some very old and important things are taking place in these vehicles. Souls are being saved, nourished, fortified and strengthened.

I'm proud to be a part of that incredible process. I'm also delighted to see that God's work continues no matter the technology, the place, the state of the economy. Souls still hunger for Him and find Him wherever they are or are going.

Of course, I realize that's not how most people view me.

Many people of the world would look upon me as a "loser." I am 74 years old, in my 75th year. I am not wealthy, or famous, or powerful. I am a common man. I am a rideshare driver.

Truth be told, this simple description of myself, what I do and my station in life, is typical of Christian servants throughout history. It has been the overlooked, forgotten and downtrodden who have carried most of the load for the Lord over the centuries. We have done this work because we were led to do it. And because we love the work, and the One who sent us.

I am your rideshare driver. But when you come into my car, and you care to visit about higher things, I am here waiting with the gift of life.

To be clear, none of the rideshare companies I have worked for endorse my personal views. I don't force them on anyone. I would never use my position or job to do that. But when the conversation suggests somebody is in need of inspiration, and they seem open to a message that might lift their spirits, my ministry on wheels is there for them.

I am your rideshare driver. And through God's grace, I hope to be, when my passengers are low or lonely, so much more.

*   *   *

It is very uplifting when someone starts speaking about issues of spirituality. Other times, I can pick up on their emotional or spiritual state and see the opportunity to encourage them, or to challenge them to draw nearer to our Lord. We are blessed to be a blessing.

I came to know these driving services would become a ministry in 2018. After discerning my job as a health-benefits adviser was not a good long-term fit, I left the field and went from driving part-time to being a full-time rideshare driver for a major, well-known company. Later, I began performing rideshare services for a second company, Envoy America. This company provides medical-transportation services in Texas and other states. I've become one of their go-to guys, counted on to drive all the way from Dallas to El Paso—an eleven-hour drive on the other side of our massive state. Sometimes I even drive all the way to Arizona.

For both companies, I am a free agent—a self-employed, independent contractor. During my years in Germany, I picked up a German term for such work: *Feuerwehr*. This translates roughly as "fire department," meaning an independent worker hired to spring into action whenever and wherever those services are required.

My many years of living in Germany and working throughout Europe have enriched and formed my character, strengthened my faith and broadened my horizons. It was there that I served in the U.S. Army, became an itinerant technical service provider, and, most importantly for my life story, met Rose.

The trauma of my first marriage seared me and still defines me. I fully understand what divorced people, believers and non-believers, must deal with as they reckon with the disintegration of a marriage and family. That tremendous pain and deeply wounded spirit would yield in time to finding my second and current wife, Roswitha, or the name our family and friends call her, Rose. My soulmate, Rose is my "Gypsy woman," born of a German mother and Romanian father.

These experiences and others give us empathy, and more importantly, love. My mobile ministry allows me to reach out to people, find out where they are in their spiritual lives, and try to lift them up. My little church on wheels is, in this sense, a rolling "love boat." Considering that I am playing classical music throughout my driving, I think the term "Serenity Chamber on Wheels" may be more accurate. I find classical music calms the nerves, creating tranquility and serenity in the midst of life's stress, traffic, noise and chaos.

My work provides the opportunity to counsel, communicate, share, intercede, and assist. Amidst these activities, sometimes I perform other services to show my love for others. These include giving occasional free rides for those in need. Sometimes I help jump-start a stalled vehicle. Occasionally I report suspicious activity I observe to the police.

The best part of driving is meeting new people from all over the world. With these customers, I may have an opportunity to share, pray, counsel, give thanks and rejoice in serving the kingdom of God.

I never try to force myself or my beliefs on others. I generally listen patiently to determine, from their words and body language, if they are open to spiritual things. Sometimes I say something to "break the ice" and see how they respond. I surely need to pray and fast more to be even more effective in these efforts.

For those passengers interested in talking—and not all are—I strive to be a holy vessel of friendliness, goodness and Christ-like love. It's not infrequent for people to open up and start sharing about their lives. I've had people ask me for personal counsel, for prayer. I've asked others if they wish to allow me to share my insights and/or pray for them.

In the end I trust the Holy Spirit to guide me and help me discern if passengers are open to the gospel and the message of our Lord. As I am led, when I see an open door to encourage and share, I enter it.

A few examples give an idea of my work. Some of these encounters have grown into lasting relationships and friendships.

A few years ago I met Kris, a young Black man from Plano, Texas, a large suburb of Dallas. Kris was himself an evangelist. He tried to lead rideshare drivers over to Christ. He started preaching to me! It turned into a joyful conversation after he asked me my thoughts about death. I responded I preferred to talk about life. And so it went. We became friends. As often as possible we meet up for coffee, tea, breakfast, or a meal.

Another passenger I remember is Derek, a young Black man who was also involved in ridesharing. Derek said his father drove ride share and I felt encouraged to ask him to have his father contact me regarding sharing a hybrid vehicle (ride share rental). This would cut the cost of driving in half, considerably increasing the profit margin. A week or so later Shane would contact me. He was himself an evangelist about my age. After explaining my proposal with him we began sharing our ride share rental vehicle. As time went on we became close friends, encouraging one another and sharing our driving experiences and life lessons learned. Both of us gained from the relationship and continue sharing spiritual things today over three years later.

On another occasion I picked up a young woman who made it clear she was seeking a Biblical, Christ-centered assembly or congregation. I shared my desire to find the same thing. I recommended a church in the Dallas area where I had been welcomed. It is a very diverse and Christ-centered congregation. She was very grateful and we had a joyful conversation.

More recently I picked up a young lady at a hospital and took her home back out into the middle of nowhere in west Texas. During this trip we had beautiful conversations about the love of the gospel and what the Father has shared with us.

A young man named Terry hailed me from Oak Cliff, a neighborhood of Dallas. He needed a ride to Denton, a suburb about an hour north. He was very excited and shared a spiritual awakening he had just experienced. I rejoiced and encouraged him.

In all these and countless other conversations like them, the Holy Spirit has led people sharing a common vehicle towards a common destination: His Holy Presence and His Peace.

The most rewarding conversations are those that show a passenger has been saved. This doesn't happen often during a short ride. Still, seeds often are sown there that grow later. Because I rarely stay in touch with my passengers after I drop them off, I seldom know about this good fruit. But I've no doubt it happens. I feel God lets me know my efforts are productive and not in vain. The good will that can lead to such grace is obvious to me in the joy they show as they leave my vehicle, after a conversation praising and seeking God.

It's become clear to me that ridesharing, organized by apps and phones, is just the most recent form of transportation that allows the drivers to reach people spiritually. In days past there were wagons, stagecoaches, trains, ships. Now we minister in greater comfort and speed but with the same opportunities to reach souls. Come to think of it, maybe Phillip was kind of a stowaway when he jumped on the wagon with the Ethiopian eunuch and shared the gospel! To be a modern-day Phillip is the highest of honors I can aspire to.

I believe we are all sojourners in this land, all of us aliens. American Indian blood flows through me, just as gypsy blood flows through my German bride. Maybe these traits guide some of us onward also. I do feel that I am a trailblazer of sorts, bringing new spiritual life and activity to a zone of our economy that needs it.

Christ was crucified with His arms wide open. Our Father showed us that He wants us to receive His love, and in so doing die to self. We must give forgiveness to receive it. My own life experience has revealed to me that forgiveness becomes reality when we no longer hurt from what people have done to us, but rather we hurt for the people who did it to us. The wounded soul has been healed when true forgiveness is fulfilled in Christ and in us Christ eternally. We must repent and do away with our bitterness.

That is the message I believe the Lord has given me to share with the world: "Come home to Papa! Let me squeeze the devil out of you, the selfishness and the sin, and fill you with my love!" I like to call it a "holy hug." In His arms is where I received a meaningful, productive life after my own Damascus Road experience following the end of my first marriage.

This isn't to gloss over the more difficult parts of the job. We deal with customers who are drunk, either partying or just trying to forget their troubles. Sometimes they make a mess, vomiting in my car.

Other customers can be rude or unfair. Some are just difficult, cantankerous. I remind myself when I experience these things that these are the children of God who need to know His love the most. Simply put, we need to be children of the light, growing to become warriors of the light. If then we are filled with the light Jesus shares with us, we must share it with our brothers and sisters!

With these more challenging customers and others, I try to be sensitive and meet them where they're at. Sometimes we share the gospel most effectively by showing somebody who is anxious or hurting a quiet act of selflessness and decency, rather than reaching out with words.

I've faced other challenges, as well. Since the Covid restrictions were put in place a few years ago, I've found many gas stations no longer offer restrooms to their customers. I don't know if this is to avoid health problems with the authorities or to lower maintenance or labor costs. Still, filling up one's tank with gas only to find the men's room closed afterwards is not a welcome development!

Though I'm not literally a cowboy riding the range on a horse, my work does require a trusty steed of sorts. I've had a "stable" full of vehicles to allow me to do my work. Almost a dozen personal cars have served me during these past eight years, plus many rental vehicles. A number of these vehicles have been lost in the line of duty, unfortunate casualties of collisions—part of the dangerous side of my profession.

I like to say I've had four horses shot out from under me in the last two years. That is to say, I've gone through four different vehicles due to accidents.

This body count, by the way, does not include Blackie, my 1998 Mercedes, which I had spent $3,000 restoring. I lent it to Alfred, a Christian brother whose wedding I had officiated, who then drove it into the front of a Dollar Tree store in Bedford, Texas. He called to tell me excitedly that God had spared him injury; Alfred was less concerned about the vehicle, which was totaled. After scolding me for loaning the vehicle to Alfred, his wife left several hundred dollars with my brother, then the two left town.

Goldie was a 2007 gold Camry I owned for a while. It was destroyed in December 2020 on Highway 75 near Walnut Hill. A car passed me at high speed, then attempted to exit the highway where there was no exit. I attempted to avoid the wayward vehicle but it quickly drifted over and hit the right front corner of my car, pushing me into the center retaining wall. The force of the accident crushed the brake actuator in my car and broke the engine block.

Whitey was a white 2010 Prius rental. In March 2021, a young man turned into my left front fender at the intersection of Forest and I-635. I learned afterwards he had been removed from his father's insurance following a series of other accidents.

Next to fall in the line of duty was Red, my 2014 red Prius. Red met its fate in August 2022 in Balch Springs, when a white ¾ ton pickup hit my right front fender with its extended rear tires. The collision whipped me around 90 degrees. His truck spun like a top, turning around 180 degrees before coming to a rest in the middle of a school crossing.

Most recently, in October 2022 I was the victim of a hit-and-run that occurred on a Saturday night in Grand Prairie, Texas. A gray SUV hit my left rear, causing severe damage to the fender and ruining the tire. The driver sped away, running a red light, before I could identify them. My passenger was kind enough to help me change the damaged tire. I delivered him to his destination with the temporary "donut" tire before I parked my disabled vehicle for the night and weekend.

Throughout these adventures, I've battled not only inattentive drivers and serious danger but also unfair insurance companies. Such is life for a rideshare driver. Yet through it all God has preserved me! I have always managed to find another horse to keep going.

I've spoken of higher things here to share my motivations in my work. Yet obviously much of my attention must be devoted to driving: the roads, the signage, other drivers, bumps in the road. I try to make the ride as comfortable as possible for my passengers.

These are some thoughts from this simple rideshare cowboy.

The sights that fly past my current vehicle as I do my work are familiar to many. The skyline of downtown Dallas has changed since it became internationally known 40 years ago when featured in the intro to the TV series "Dallas." It is larger now, and still towering. We see it now as the backdrop to televised Dallas Cowboys games (still known as "America's Team").

I drive through and around the Dallas downtown almost every day. It's the center of a beating heart of people and commerce that has become the fastest growing metropolitan area in the United States. Here, there's no shortage of people to minister to.

Leaving downtown, I'll pull out onto a highway that leads to the many sprawling suburbs, exurbs, and small towns in north Texas. These experiences are usually a gorgeous background that's too easy to take for granted. Amidst the beautiful sunrises and sunsets, constant buzz of new construction, occasionally violent thunderstorms, and the steady change in weather and season, I drive. During occasional torrential rains, the roads can turn into rivers and lakes, making me feel more like the captain of a ship on the high seas. I am always amazed by the wonders of God's creation.

There is much work to be done here to bring others to see this glory more fully.

Chapter One

Memories

"Thank you, sir. And keep fighting the old fight."

Passenger review on rideshare app, given to the author

What is the state of our lives and souls today? What is truly on our minds? What troubles and motivates us?

I suggest rideshare drivers are some of your best experts at answering these questions. We might even be better sources of information than public-opinion polls. People let their guard down when conversing with a driver they will never see again. For this reason, I think I have my finger pretty firmly on the public pulse.

I will begin each of my chapters with a quote from one of my passengers. They're asked to review me and their experience at the end of every ride. Right now, I have a rating of 4.94 out of 5 stars. I've provided more than 19,000 rides for well over 30,000 passengers in 8 years of ridesharing. These quotes are offered not to "puff up" my vanity. Believe me, I've done any number of things during those 19,000-plus rides that can make me blush in embarrassment! I offer them to show my goal is to create such an experience in my passengers. I believe it's a worthy goal. And maybe I will give a little inspiration to you as you deal with the people who enter your life during the day.

I will share some meditations that come to me as I drive in the hope that you find them helpful. I am no Billy Graham, Derek Prince or David Wilkerson. But I share a few insights that have come to me from many years of working with people, including those who share their very souls with somebody who will leave their life as soon as they exit the vehicle.

Now, I'd like to share with you how my ministry on wheels reaches people. I think the best way to do this is to talk about the things that are on people's minds. These are the subjects that come up freely while I'm sharing a conversation with somebody on the way to the rider's destination.

These are the main areas of my ministry. To be clear, when I say "ministry," I am an undercover ordained minister. I am a simple servant of Christ. But I believe all of us, who truly seek to serve Him and share the gospel regularly, have a personal ministry. Mine happens to be conducted in a rideshare vehicle.

I try to break the ice with my passengers in various ways. I do try to share my faith while respecting their independence and choices. I will do whatever it takes as long as it doesn't require coercion or sin.

Originally God spoke everything into existence. I am, of course, far more limited in my conversational skills. I've found a conversation of substance usually requires a ride time of around half an hour.

Most passengers are open to conversation. And most are open to talking about faith. Obviously if I pick up more than one passenger for a ride, it is less likely the conversation will include me.

Usually I say something to get the conversation started. I try to be as honest and nonjudgmental as possible. I feel genuine faith means doing good in the shadow of the Father and meeting people where they're at

Do we need to approach people about the gospel in a way different from how the early Christians did it? It's hard to say how exactly people shared the gospel in the early days of the church. I've found it to be most effective when we show respect for one another and that we value every individual as an equal. I think transparency and vulnerability are required prerequisites to be really effective.

We show others we are truly listening to them by showing genuine sympathy and empathy. Telling people "I know this about the Bible and you don't" – that is not humble or effective. In our conversations with the lost or the searching, we must shine the light of Christ, not push people away.

You might call this the evangelism of friendship or conversation. All I know is that it's important for me to build a relationship with people so that I can talk to them about the most important relationship there is: the one with our Father in Heaven and with Christ Jesus, our Lord and Savior.

These efforts can be a little tricky. If I don't see an open window, a receptive ear, I leave them alone. I believe we need to be humble and not invade their private space. I believe current outreach efforts too often ignore this requirement. But I also believe that when that opportunity presents itself, to meaningfully interact and share the Word of God and Christ's love, it is our duty to act.

Early Christians who ministered to the sick and dying were called "Parabolani," or "risk takers." I believe I am a modern-day Parabolanus. Rideshare drivers have been shot, stabbed, run over, threatened with road rage, spit on, exposed to contagious diseases, and endangered in other ways. I accept these risks to do my job and share my faith. I believe we must love God and people and boldly serve Christ Jesus where we are called.

One important way I connect with my passengers is to share experiences we have in common. Something that comes up regularly is what I would put together until the topic of memories. All of us carry with us memories of our lives to date. These memories shape who we are. Many are good memories. Some memories haunt us. All come up in some manner in conversation, and light a pathway to the person's soul.

This is especially true of the passengers I specialize in driving. I've branched out and chauffeur not just passengers in my personal vehicle for a rideshare company, but also larger groups of seniors. The company I work for asks us to be more than just a driver, but also a companion. I try to do this the best way I can. And they have many memories.

*   *   *

I was born in Glendale, Arizona, in 1948. My parents, Herman and Martha Beshears, were married there on January 1, 1948. Dad was originally from the Red River Valley between Texas and Oklahoma. While the name Beshears is of French origin (a variation of "brewer"), my family also has American Indian ancestors, probably Choctaw or something similar from the Oklahoma and north Texas territories. Cajun and/or Creole blood also is part of my DNA.

My parents owned a baby Blue 1950 Ford and an Airstream mobile home. We lived in the latter on my paternal grandparents' property until moving to Arizona. My father took a job at Goodyear plant there. Once there he purchased a piece of land in Buckeye, Arizona, and built a house on it. As I turned eight years old my dad allowed me to help him dig up a tree stump in the yard to earn a little spending money. From the leftover material at the Goodyear rubber plant where they worked, my parents brought home what was needed to construct a small circular swimming pool—maybe three or four feet deep and 15 feet wide. It was big enough to provide welcome relief from the blistering summers there.

A few years later they sold the house in Buckeye and purchased a forty-acre farm in Rainbow Valley, between Buckeye and Liberty. Our farm was soon populated with hundreds of red chickens as well as some guinea hens, pigs, peacocks and turkeys—not to mention the scorpions, snakes, rabbits and other animals that roamed our property before we arrived.

Looking back, I can see that when I attended school in Liberty, several things happened that affected my emotional development. Besides being, at one point, the smallest boy in my class, I was lefthanded. This natural orientation was nevertheless frowned upon at the time. My teachers weren't willing to help me learn to effectively use my left hand, so they forced me to learn writing using my right hand. Looking back, I don't blame my teachers and think their attitudes were simply products of their time and environment.

Other factors impacted my personality. I was required to repeat third grade. Also, I was a bedwetter. All of these adversities imprinted themselves on my personality. Poor coordination, low self-esteem, no longtime friends, individualism—these were byproducts of my youth. I committed to memory Ralph Waldo Emerson's adage, which lifted my spirits: "Whoso would be a man, must be a nonconformist." I also picked up another adage that stuck with me: "The only way to have a friend is to be one."

There were plenty of happier memories. In school I played the back rear half of Rudolph the Red-Nosed Reindeer in the Christmas play. I also recall learning the story of "The Little Engine that Could" and repeated his signature line: "I know I can, I know I can, I know I can."

Other memories from our time in the Grand Canyon State still stand out. I remember watching the fireworks on the Fourth of July and New Year's over the mountains to our east near Phoenix. My family went to a drive-in movie theater to watch the movie *The Ten Commandments* starring Charlton Heston. There are many other random but pleasant memories from this time: playing mini-golf at a course in Phoenix, which featured waterfalls as well as obstacles such as tunnels and cliffs; deer hunting trips with my father and his friends; eating pomegranates; visiting the Grand Canyon and Carlsbad Caverns; going fishing with my father; touring the old Yuma Prison.

Another memory that lingers is of a primitive form of transportation in which I engaged frequently: walking. We walked a great deal in those days as children. We walked freely, to catch the school bus or just to enjoy the great outdoors. Another vivid memory is walking through the woods, countryside, and desert landscape, which was traversed by dry river beds that sometimes were filled with surging, dangerous water during flash floods.

A certain peculiar memory I have is of snakes. We made sure to steer clear of snakes. Scripture shows us in the Garden of Eden that we should avoid snakes! We had to cover our chicken pen on all sides with wire to keep them out. We had a chicken farm and we had hundreds of chickens to fellowship with. I had to walk about a half a mile to the main road to catch a bus to school. Sometimes I made a point of walking in the middle of the dirt road to avoid the bushes where I heard the angry rattles of rattlesnakes.

We moved often. This was in large part so that my mother could be near her sister (my aunt). I never set down roots anywhere. I felt like a nomad without a tribe. Christ would become my safe haven.

As we traveled between Arizona and Texas, I would sleep on one of the seats and my brother would sleep on the luggage rack. When he was very young, he would sleep in my mother's arms.

In the summer of 1957, after my father was laid off from Goodyear, we moved again—to my father's home state of Texas. Though born in Arizona, my memories run through the Lone Star State, which I've long called home. We Texans are a unique breed. Sometimes I think we're the most unusual collection of people on the planet. My background helps to explain not only how I came to be a rideshare driver in greater Dallas, but the experiences that led me to use my vehicle for a ministry on wheels.

Much of what shapes how I treat my passengers is the Southern hospitality I grew up with. Unfortunately, during the last few decades, it's become much more difficult to find the hospitality and simple courtesy we practiced back in the 1950s and 1960s. That's when I came of age.

Another random memory involved race relations, a topic that soon began to consume the nation. In fourth grade, I learned, and repeated at home, that all men were created equal. I learned this view conflicted with that of my mother. This was evidenced years later after my return from Germany, when I gave a young Black man a ride with my sister in the car. My mother later asked me if I wanted my sister to marry a Black man! My father, who had served in the Army, did not express the same views.

It's funny how you remember the food. During my visits to my mother's family in Kentucky, we enjoyed a wealth of old-fashioned canned foods. The food I was most fond of were the sauerkraut-filled banana peppers and thin candied yams, rather than the huge sweet potatoes we know primarily today. They were a little bit stringy but crispy and tasty. My favorite food as a child was the tamales that were made by our Hispanic brethren in our Nazarene church. I enjoyed a hayride sponsored by our church, after which we would roast hot dogs and marshmallows over an open fire.

And there were the home-cooked meals: bacon and spicy sausage; luscious gravy that was medium brown with a lot of milk and some flour; billowy buttermilk biscuits; and desserts featuring my grandmother's fantastic pies: pecan, pumpkin and my favorite, chocolate (French-style, rich chocolate pudding with browned-egg white meringue topping and light flaky crust bottom). We would all get together as a family on a big kitchen table and have breakfast together.

My early spiritual journey was woven through these memories. I grew up attending church and was surrounded by the supportive Christian ethos that pervades the South. We later attended a Nazarene church in Buckeye, Arizona. There I was baptized when I was around eight years old (I don't recall exactly, as memories can be imperfect at that age). My brother Don and I during this time began to take on our dual roles: I sought to be the "good son," Don would cut up and be "bad," apparently seeking attention.

I remember vividly how my brother Don continued his descent into troublemaking, becoming the black sheep of the family. Because my parents were often absent from the home, this undermined my relationship with my brother in two ways. First, Don rebelled to gain attention from our often-absent parents. Second, I inherited the task of taking care of my three siblings. My taking on the role of a third parent created tension between us that should not have existed.

Before this time, Don and I had been so close that people thought we were twins. In part, this was because our parents often dressed us alike, buying us the same attire. I remember wearing a mustard yellow polo T-shirt with medium brown trim and colored pocket trim with Levis heavyweight jeans, belt and cowboy hat. My brother wore the same thing. Unfortunately, the experiences of our childhood drove a wedge between Don and me, destroying a formerly strong bond.

One memory above all stands out from my youth. I was attending R.L. Turner High School in Carrollton (a Dallas suburb) on November 22, 1963, when President Kennedy was shot and killed right there in nearby Dallas. I learned of this in my math class. I saw the live news forecast when Jack Ruby shot Lee Harvey Oswald.

We moved often, and I remember many periods of being alone, without friends. Later, my mother would suffer a nervous breakdown and be institutionalized in the state mental hospital in Terrell, Texas. There were many such difficult memories.

But God has a way of making the pretty ones crowd out the negative ones, if we only give Him half a chance to show us the joy and beauty of our lives.

*　　　　*　　　　*

I've come to believe memories are powerful tools God uses to guide and inspire us. His Holy Word makes clear the importance of memories.

In fact, his Holy Word instructs us to remember certain things:

"I will remember the deeds of the LORD; yes, I will remember your miracles of long ago. I will consider all your works and meditate on all your mighty deeds." (Psalm 77:11-12)

Other things we remember because they are right and good for us to remember:

"I will give thanks to the Lord with my whole heart; I will recount all of your wonderful deeds." (Psalm 9:1)

"You may say to yourselves, 'These nations are stronger than we are. How can we drive them out?' But do not be afraid of them; remember well what the Lord your God did to Pharaoh and to all Egypt. You saw with your own eyes the great trials, the signs and wonders, the mighty hand and outstretched arm, with which the Lord your God brought you out. The Lord your God will do the same to all the peoples you now fear." (Deuteronomy 7:17–19)

It's also beneficial to honor people who set good examples:

"The righteous man will be remembered forever." (Psalm 112:6)

And there are the teachings of Jesus Christ and our duty to remember His final hours:

"...The Lord Jesus, on the night he was betrayed, took bread, and when he had given thanks, he broke it and said, 'This is my body, which is for you; do this in remembrance of me.'" (1 Corinthians 11:23-24)

Sometimes, of course, it is better for us to forget:

"But one thing I do: Forgetting what is behind and straining toward what is ahead, I press on toward the goal to win the prize for which God has called me heavenward in Christ Jesus." (Philippians 3:13-14)

*   *   *

Now you know a little about me and the memories I carry, memories that shape who I am and how I treat others. I'll share with you now a few stories of my passengers, and will share a lot more later. These give an idea of how memories, the mental building blocks of our lives, shape who we are, how we act and what we believe.

The following are some recent stories.

I pulled alongside a large industrial building in Oak Cliff, part of Dallas. The structure appeared to be an IT center. The woman who came out was Black, in her thirties. Alice needed a ride home.

We talked of many things. How fear is gripping the government and us. How such fear can be blasphemy. Much of what we discussed came down to comparing memories, which were road signs of our faith journeys.

I told her of my time in Germany, where I was stationed in the U.S. Army and which became my home away from home. Alice told me of how her grandmother taught her the importance of her faith. She noted her grandmother said the church is supposed to be a "bride without spot or wrinkle." The church should not be weak or cowed by social agendas.

Our sharing of stories ended well. At the end she expressed great gratitude for the Lord bringing us together. We were sharing our faith, building up one another in a common service of Christ. It was as

Paul said: we must relate to one another. It was very uplifting for both of us, and both of us admitted so.

I found it fascinating and revealing that Alice's memories of her grandmother sustain and guide her spiritually to this day.

It was midnight in the northeast Dallas area near the suburb of Richardson when I picked up Deidre. A student at Abilene Christian University, she was needing a ride to the small town of Farmersville, a rural community as the name suggests on the outer periphery of the Dallas metroplex. Deidre plied me with all kinds of questions. As is often the case, our conversation began with a question about my wife Rose, whose picture can be seen on my phone. I spoke of Rose, and Germany, and how her lovely name was common in Germany.

We spoke of how we got to know each other from the inside out. And I shared the pain I had suffered in my first marriage, which ended in betrayal, humiliation and divorce. I could tell it made an impression. She was at the age of trying to sort out relationships and walk through the landmines that our culture sets before young people trying to find the right member of the opposite sex. When we parted forty minutes later, the hard memories seared into me all those years ago in Germany seemed to help guide her as she starts out in life.

In the eastern suburb of Sachse, I picked up Mehmet. He was playing basketball with his eight-year-old girl and nine-year-old boy. They were going to a nearby tire shop. I noticed immediately how well-behaved Mehmet's children were. The boy picked up the $1 million "bill" I had left in the back seat to spark conversation (more about that later). He read the text and asked me questions. I gave one to his little sister also.

Mehmet was very congenial and didn't interrupt when I explained, in response to his boy's questions, "I am sharing my riches." He told his children to thank me as they left.

What to make of this encounter? This will sow seeds for him and his children, memories of an old man kindly showing them the keys to the Kingdom of God.

Clement was waiting for me in Fort Worth. His wife was in the hospital, expecting a baby. On this joyous occasion, I shared not only spiritual matters but also practical advice about becoming a rideshare driver and the opportunities that presents. I gave him my card and information on how I could help him join the business if he wished.

A native of Cameroon, Clement left full of hope, for the future of his family and his career. I don't know what became of him, but I know the memories forged there talking of Jesus Christ, his new baby, and hope for a new job and future were received with great gladness and an open heart. For me, that is a spiritual home run.

Chapter Two

Work

"He's just a gentleman. A real gentleman."

In my work and ministry, I find I have three reliable icebreakers to get the conversation going.

One is the fact that I've lived in Germany. That fact is noted in my driver profile.

The second is a photo of my dear wife, Rose. I'll talk about her and the power of her photo—the screensaver on my phone—in the next chapter.

The third is a small rectangular flyer that looks like a $1 million dollar bill. I often deliberately leave it in the back seat. When passengers sit down, they can't help but notice it. Other times I hand one to a passenger, often when they leave.

On the back of what looks like a $1 million bill is a powerful testimony about Jesus and the importance of salvation in His name. But I take things a step at a time.

When somebody asks me—as they regularly do—about the $1 million bill, I respond: "A penny for your thoughts, a million for your heart." This icebreaker catches people's attention, since we all value money and what it stands for. And it prompts conversations that can lead a passenger who just wanted a ride to an earthly destination to find the road to Paradise.

This technique comes naturally to me. For one thing, I like to share. It may sound like preaching sometimes, but it's really just my trying to give away the goodness I've found in Jesus Christ.

For those less inclined to share the gospel, such outreach might seem intimidating, even daunting. They prefer to avoid such work. I understand. It's not for everyone. For me, though, it's second nature.

This is at the core of my work. Driving is what I do to earn a living. Sharing the wonders and mysteries of God's Kingdom is what I do as an integral part of my job so I can one day report to my Master I did what I could to lead people unto Him.

On the subject of work: That is a major reason why people hail a rideshare. In fact, during the hours I work, most of my passengers are going to or from work. I'd estimate 50 percent fall into this category, while another 20 percent are going to or from the airport on work-related business. On the weekends, that number flips, as the vast majority of customers are out on personal time and pursuing pleasure in some way.

This makes sense, of course. We must work to support ourselves. God requires work of us. Idle time is the devil's workshop, as they say. I can attest to this, as the people who use my services on weekends tend to be out for a pleasant time amidst the nightlife of the Dallas area—and too often are up to no good.

In my own life and work, I put in my time to earn my daily bread and then some. It's not unusual for me to work 12 hours at a stretch, logging up to 36 trips during that time and driving 300 and up to 500 miles.

Staying busy can become a way of not dealing with life, or our relationships or personal situations that are troubling. I try to stay busy but to do work needed to support myself and my family.

This work of ferrying people to their own jobs is rewarding because I help people provide for themselves and pursue their career goals. And it gives me a chance to share my heart and acts of kindness to strangers, share my riches and hand out more fake $1 million bills. I have had people come back to my car asking where I got them so that they could share them as well.

I am able to relate to people from all walks of life. I've done many things, held many jobs, pursued a number of professions. I've found God has given me a talent to hold up my end of the conversation with virtually anyone who enters my vehicle and chooses to engage in conversation. It's a talent and a blessing I seek to use for His glory.

*   *   *

My father was a hard-working, simple man. While in high school (which he did not complete), his life took an abrupt turn. On a summer night in 1944, he was arrested after joyriding with some friends in a stolen car. He was given the choice of incarceration or military service during World War II. He took the latter, joining the Army. My father was then sent to the Pacific theater, and eventually transferred to the Philippines after being wounded. After shooting a Filipino caught stealing while on guard duty, he was sent back to the United States and honorably discharged. He would meet and marry my mother on January 1, 1948.

Like the greatest example of a humble worker ever put before us, our Lord and Savior, my dad learned to be a carpenter. He moved through a succession of jobs and careers during his life, and his family would move with him. Factory worker for Goodyear; door-to-door salesman for the Fuller Brush Company; owner of a janitorial-supply company—those are a few of his career hitches. My father was a very successful salesman, winning several trophies for his work in the Dallas-Fort Worth area. Eventually he became a field manager for the Fuller Brush Company in Paris, Texas, so we moved there. He did not find the same success in Paris, a small town in a relatively impoverished rural area. He suffered from sugar diabetes, passing out once while driving.

My mother was creative and miscast as a housewife and mother. She didn't have much interest in this, later taking a job at the Goodyear plant and often neglecting things at home. I suspect my father submitted to her desires because she had a better education than he (Dad dropped out in the tenth grade), and simply because he loved his wife. She was a bit taller than my father, which made for a somewhat awkward scene when they walked together. I stepped up and helped fill the domestic role left void at home by my mother's frequent absence.

Because of my father's troubles in providing for us, there were many moves over a ten-year period. After we returned from Arizona to Texas, I lived in a series of towns: Farmers Branch, Carrollton (North Dallas), Paris, Longview, Pine Tree, Denison. I remember working the fields outside Paris for "eight bits" ($1 an hour), picking tomatoes and cucumbers until the end of summer. Later that summer the wages dropped to 75 cents an hour, yet I continued to do the work. I entered a training program for mechanics working at a local tool-rental store, and in electronics at a local TV repair shop. My interest in practical tinkering would remain throughout my life.

I took various jobs during this time as I found my way in life. I worked for the Texas Department of Public Safety, where I assisted with quality control for paving roads. I replaced old cross ties on a railroad to Perrin Air Force Base (now closed) outside Denison. Afterwards, I attended Grayson Community College, where I studied Electronics Technology. In early 1969 I was let go from a co-op program at Texas Instruments because of low grades. I left college and soon received a draft notice. After failing the initial physical I was retested and allowed to join. The Army sent me to Fort Bliss in El Paso for basic training. Upon being tested the

Army was sufficiently impressed by my aptitude scores that they asked me to become an officer. Not wishing to make a career of it, I declined.

The Army did not send me to Southeast Asia. It may have been because my younger brother Don was already there. Instead, they sent me to the Army's finance school at Fort Benjamin Harrison in Indiana. I became a specialist in the finance corps.

The Army's next decision would change the whole focus of my life. For while I would not become a career soldier, I would become a sojourner in foreign lands. The Army sent me to Europe. It would become my home for most of my life.

The first of my divine appointments in Europe was in Heidelberg, Germany. I was stationed there and assigned to Central Finance and Accounting Office Europe. Once there, I had free time and visited downtown Heidelberg and the archaic castle on the Neckar River.

Soon I was detached to Karlsruhe, Germany. Karlsruhe is a university city and the seat of the German Supreme Court. I didn't realize at the time that this German city would become more of a home to me than Arizona or Texas ever had been. There I was to replace the clerk who had gone AWOL after befriending antiwar students and gaining a girlfriend at the nearby university.

I worked in a three-man office. I was responsible for maintaining the archives of Central Finance and Accounting. My work included being a secretary, company clerk, archivist, cashier, bookkeeper, records keeper, and driver—all for this three-man office. The funding division was responsible for providing American currency (bills and coins) for the U.S. military community and funds for government and military offices throughout the Eastern Hemisphere.

My days there were typical of American soldiers overseas. We worked hard and played hard. I am not proud of some of the "play": I recall having my first Bacardi cola and getting drunk; I joined some soldiers who made it to the red-light district (I waited outside the establishment). I had much growing up to do.

Though I wasn't in combat, my time in Germany was not free of danger. A Marxist terrorist cell known as the Baader-Meinhof Gang bombed the base where I was stationed. The explosion damaged buildings and the car of one of my friends. Fortunately I was off base at the time.

The Army offered me over $10,000 to reenlist. But I had no intention of staying in Germany. My goal was to return to the United States with the German woman I hoped would become my wife (more about that later). Upon leaving the Army, I returned to Texas. I went back to live in Denison and enrolled at Grayson County College, waiting for my fiancé to join me. When she did not come, I returned to Germany and took various jobs there, which later included assignments at sites throughout Europe. Like my father, I was good at and interested in a variety of trades. Because of my romantic and later family relationships, I remained in Europe for many years.

I came to love Germany. The Germans are great at keeping things clean. They're orderly, tidy, hard-working problem-solvers. Each time they have gone through a horrendous major war, the Germans have cleaned up the mess, removed the rubble and rebuilt their country.

One of my favorite memories from my time in the Army was my assignment to East Germany as part of a goodwill tour. During a week-long stay in Berlin, I spent half a day in East Berlin on the other side of the Iron Curtain. We traveled there by military train and were required to wear civilian clothes. I took film in my camera and snapped some photos of the Olympic Stadium and other sites. However, I was soon besieged by curious East Germans who had never seen a Polaroid camera, and who asked me to take their picture. I did so, thinking I could easily go and buy some more Polaroid film at a local store. That didn't work out well, as such goods were not readily available. I ended up giving my film away. Still, I suppose that was the purpose of the goodwill tour. I tried to do my best to create goodwill that would burst forth with many others when the Berlin Wall came down many years later.

My favorite German foods include *Rouladen* (thinly sliced lean beef served with a dill pickle and onion), *Spätzle* (noodles like a dumpling), and *Sauerbraten* (roast beef marinated in red wine. Of course, I enjoyed their potatoes also, which the Germans called *Erdapfel* (literally "earth apple"). In my travels, I was a sucker for *gulasch*, which was popular in south central Europe and into the Balkans.

I've visited almost every European country. Among the countries I've not yet been blessed to visit—but that are on my "bucket list"—are Portugal, Greece, Bulgaria, Romania, Hungary, the Balkan countries of former Yugoslavia and Belarus. I've spent over half of my life in Europe. I've learned German but also some basic French, Italian and other languages to get by in my work there.

Some of my favorite countries are Germany, Switzerland, Italy, and the Czech Republic. I had my honeymoon in Paris with my first wife and enjoyed the typical tourist sites. As I left the Army and, after some time back in the States, I transitioned to a series of itinerant jobs across Europe in the private sector: installing medical equipment for Siemens Corporation, ensuring quality control for atomic power plants, troubleshooting and upgrading technical equipment. I traveled throughout the beautiful continent and experienced its greatness and its diversity.

I learned I had divine appointments there.

*   *   *

As I do my work now—which consists mostly of taking my passengers to and from their work—I am struck by the simplicity of it all. Often we glorify jobs and careers far beyond their rightful place in our lives. What's maybe worse, we exalt the career-centered types who become wealthy and influential from making work the center of their days. Christ reminds us that most of these people are in a bad place.

As I drive people to their jobs, I am reminded very directly that the stories of labor in the Bible continue in a different but similar form today. That is to say, these days, as in the Bible, most work is fairly menial. Being a rideshare driver certainly falls into that description.

That is as it should be. Our Messiah told us not to envy or copy the rich. Their hearts usually were hard, their priorities misplaced. Jesus spent his time with common folk because they were the ones receptive to His message. Somewhere along the way, with our McMansions and 401(k)s and season tickets, many of us have lost that understanding.

I find it helpful to go back to the Good Book for guidance on the proper role and importance of work in our lives.

A good general rule of thumb comes from Colossians:

"Whatever you do, work at it with all your heart, as working for the Lord, not for human masters." (Colossians 3:23)

Literally from Genesis through all Holy Scriptures, God is clear that He expects us to work. We are required to support ourselves on this earth. Even in the Garden of Eden, Adam was given work to do.

"The Lord God took the man and put him in the Garden of Eden to work it and take care of it." (Genesis 2:15)

We are not to be idle. We are instructed that "each one should carry their own load." (Galatians 6:5)

"All hard work brings a profit, but mere talk leads only to poverty." (Proverbs 14:23)

And:

"A sluggard's appetite is never filled, but the desires of the diligent are fully satisfied." (Proverbs 13:4)

"A little sleep, a little slumber, a little folding of the hands to rest— and poverty will come on you like a thief and scarcity like an armed man." (Proverbs 6:10-11)

"Anyone who has been stealing must steal no longer, but must work, doing something useful with their own hands, that they may have something to share with those in need." (Ephesians 4:28)

Plus, there is higher work that we must attend to:

"Do not work for food that spoils, but for food that endures to eternal life, which the Son of Man will give you. For on him God the Father has placed his seal of approval." (John 6:27)

"May the favor of the Lord our God rest on us; establish the work of our hands for us— yes, establish the work of our hands." (Psalm 90:17)

While I am a hard worker—even a workaholic at times—I have my struggles. Self-control outside the realm of work is one. I can eat too much and find it hard to impose self-discipline on my life. I mention this to place in perspective the importance of good work habits. Sometimes those can be overblown, for we have bad habits in other areas of our lives. I find fasting to be a good way to tackle lack of self-control when it comes to appetite, for example. Hunger has a way of getting your attention and teaching a solid lesson! As our Lord teaches us, it also draws us closer to Him.

*   *   *

As I do my work, I have to be careful. I've had the company tell me to be mindful of what I say. The suggestion is that religious conversations are frowned upon. I take their instruction in stride and continue to do what I can, consistent with the law and my moral compass, to lead passengers to Jesus Christ.

For me, though these conversations are like building a glorious temple out of the most basic and unpretentious of materials. These talks with my passengers are akin to collecting construction material one pebble at a time. By touching lives, touching hearts, and interacting with one another, we accumulate these pebbles. What we do with them becomes the test of what we do with our life.

A few notes and stories about my passengers and their work stories help to provide greater context. A large percentage of my passengers are from the Indian subcontinent, going to and from their jobs. Indians rely heavily on public transport though urban Indians plan to use personal vehicles more than in pre-pandemic times.

I've found this fact to create a special calling for me. I enjoy interacting with these passengers because I recognize the sacrifice needed to be Christian in India today. There they are persecuted, especially in rural areas. I am reaching out to people who often haven't really heard Christ's message. As someone who has been an alien in a foreign land, I have walked in their shoes for many years.

A couple of examples of passengers on their way to work, and the constructive conversations we had, give an idea of the work I do with those on their way to work.

A social-studies teacher, Jerry was traveling with three of his colleagues. They were attending a teacher conference in Dallas. I dropped him off at the Omni Hotel downtown. He took a great deal of interest in my time in Germany. We ended up talking quite a bit about health care and other issues.

This is where the small mustard seeds can be planted and their potential results shown. This teacher in our public schools, where faith has been effectively banned from teaching, found my $1 million bill fascinating. As he left my vehicle, Jerry received the bill and experience quite gratefully. He departed with what I can only describe as a God-fearful "God bless you."

I don't know what impact my conversation had with Jerry. That is true of almost all of my passengers. But any time I can have even a slight impact on sharing or affirming faith in Christ among people who can influence others—and teachers rank high on that list—I know God is using me for something important. And I am joyful.

On another occasion recently, I picked up Peter at the Dallas-Fort Worth Airport. Once again, the $1 million bill sparked a conversation. He said he "loved it." Peter was a soldier on active duty far from home. That little interaction praising and uplifting one another helped lift his spirits as he did his duty away from his loved ones. Peter thanked me and left with a big, beaming smile on his face.

Sometimes, it truly is the little things that make a bigger impact than we can imagine.

I've come to believe God wants us to keep it simple. Elaborate, lengthy sermons and condemnations aren't very effective these days. A simple interaction, informal and unscripted, does the job better. That is at least what I've found to be true.

*   *   *

I couldn't properly finish this chapter on work without noting the downsides of some passenger interactions.

Sometimes people don't treat the vehicle as they should. Since my vehicle is my means of earning a living, that is not only troubling but a handicap to making ends meet.

Unauthorized pets can be a problem and result of thoughtlessness. Our rideshare company has a specific rideshare for passengers transporting pets. Once I picked up a passenger at an apartment complex in University Park in Dallas and they ambushed me with their dog. I didn't have the heart to turn them away. My "compensation" was dog hair shed throughout the back seat. Since it was dark, I couldn't see it and learned only from other passengers, who nicely complained about it.

Some of the experiences are notably worse. All rideshare drivers of any duration have stories about, well, vomit. People who get drunk enough to require a ride home often cannot control their digestive systems. This is especially a problem on weekends during my late-night runs.

Things aren't so bad if the passenger manages to throw up on the outside of the car. This happens either by their alerting me so I can pull over or by their sticking their head out of the window before emptying their stomachs. Those disgorging their stomachs by leaning out the moving vehicle often splatter vomit along the exterior of the car. But that is much easier to clean than the inside.

Too often, the passengers vomit without telling me inside the vehicle. If they honestly report the incident, they are on the hook for a cleanup fee of over $100. As a result, sometimes they leave a present behind for the next passenger to discover, to our mutual disgust.

If I am not able to find a car wash that's open, or at least a do-it-yourself station, I'll have to stop driving until the next day. If someone has sat in their vomit, I could be obligated to pay their cleaning bill. This is obviously very unfair and frustrating. But it's a part of the job. Fortunately, it's pretty rare.

Vomiters tend to come out after midnight, having drunk too much. Mostly they are women. The general practice is they come out of bars or receptions for weddings having taken in far more alcohol than they should.

Another source of aggravation is the indecisive passenger. Believe it or not, some passengers start a trip without knowing where they want to go, or properly communicating that to their driver. Sometimes they are simply drunk.

Early in my driving career, I had a middle-aged gentleman wish to go to a particular bar or restaurant. En route he changed his mind two or three times. Then, at one point, he asked, "Where are you taking me?"

"I am taking you to the last place you told me to take you," I answered.

The passenger's behavior swung wildly. At first he became belligerent. After hearing my explanation he grew confused. Finally I turned off my clock and headed towards the location he had mentioned early on. He became my best friend, asking me to join him for a meal. I told him it was my final trip of the night and I'd have to beg off. He was disappointed. Alcohol and funny personalities can produce some strange and memorable episodes in rideshare driving.

Once I picked up a bartender and shared this story with him. His response: "You get them after we've had them."

Sometimes passengers insist on bringing their animals with them, contrary to company policies. There are specially assigned drivers who handle carrying passengers with animals. Once, a man wanted his pet to come along despite my lack of designation as a driver who transports animals. The man tried to get around the policy by referring to his dog—without appropriate supporting paperwork—as a "support animal." The man was apparently homeless. I ended up taking him and his dog anyhow, and he ranted and raved much of the time. I dropped him off near a restaurant outside an airport in Addison. I believe he slept in a field nearby.

The worst scenario is when passengers falsely accuse me. I always wonder if they do so in retaliation for my sharing the Word with my passengers. It's impossible to say.

It may be as simple as passengers wanting something for nothing. When people make false accusations, the company often will give them a free ride to smooth things over as a matter of corporate policy. This of course encourages more false accusations. But those are the rules, written presumably to help the company instead of the drivers.

One person accused me, incredibly, of drinking and driving. Another said I wasn't wearing a mask during the time of Covid restrictions. One woman falsely accused me of making a pass at her. Sometimes the company withdraws driving privileges from the accused driver until they can investigate. Often the rideshare company refunds the fees paid by the accuser whether or not they are telling the truth. In this case, I lost more than a week of work because of her false charge. These false claims are not only hurtful but cost me money and the opportunity to minister to people.

Those things hurt. But they are well worth the opportunity to work in an area I love. And we are told that we will suffer for sharing the gospel.

If that's the worst thing that happens to me for ministering to people in the course of my work, I am a blessed man indeed.

Chapter 3

Love

"He even made sure I safely got to the elevator foyer of my apartment complex"

The question that passengers ask me most often is: Is that your wife?

When they ask, they are referring to the photo of my beautiful bride back in Germany. Her name is Roswitha but she goes by Rose. Her photo is on my phone, which I display in a phone cradle at the front of my vehicle.

They then ply me with more questions.

How did you meet? Where? How long have you been married?

The people asking me about Rose usually are women. They want to learn more about how we met and stayed together for so long. A typical response is what a woman recently told me after I shared about my marriage: "That gives me hope." She, like so many, is looking for the right man to marry.

Women and men both compliment Rose. The photo on my phone is so vivid, people sometimes halt themselves from talking when they see it. They think I'm in the middle of a Facetime conversation with her. Rose is a beautiful woman who is nine years younger than I, and has aged gracefully.

The commitment we've made to one another impresses people, particularly women. They are encouraged by the example of a faithful husband who loves his wife and shows off a photo of her to the world. Deep down, almost all people hope to gain this blessing. So many relationships don't last.

What these passengers don't realize—because I can't share this burden with them—is that my marriage to Rose came after many years of terrible heartache, betrayal, and spiritual pain. I share my story here because it helps to make clear my belief in the importance and glory of love and its ability to overcome anything. As Paul wrote in 1 Corinthians 13, "Love never fails."

As I mentioned before, the Army sought to keep me in the Finance Corps. However, love interfered with my professional plans. It would take me many years, and boundless personal pain, for me to realize and admit that this love was unrequited. By then, I had spent a large part of my life as a fool for love—that is to say, what I thought was love.

In the process of learning I was mistaken about my first marriage, I've learned a great deal about the true meaning of love.

* * *

It's unusual for an American citizen to divide his time between the United States and an adopted country. Yet that is what I've done for my entire adult life. The reason is simple. Both of the women I loved were German.

I met my first wife, Krimhilde, at a café/disco called Romantika in 1970. I would drink and dance, or dance and drink—I don't recall the order now. We danced a few times and went out to different clubs together.

We began dating. I assumed we were dating exclusively at that time, but looking back I am not sure. I later became aware that she had a German boyfriend who was in the German Army. I believe they were engaged. At some point she had to choose between him and me. She chose me, breaking up with him, possibly for the simple reason that I had a car and he didn't.

After we'd been dating for about a year and a half, I was transferred back to Heidelberg for my job. I spent many weekends driving between there and Karlsruhe, the city where Krimhilde lived, to visit her.

Over time, I fell hopelessly in love with her. Candidly, our having sexual relations during this time contributed to my misreading her feelings and intentions. Some say women are the only ones who make this mistake, confusing sex with a desire for commitment from their partner. But I made this mistake too, and persisted in this illusion for many years.

We talked of a wedding and moving together to the United States after I finished my military service in Europe.

When my enlistment period in the Army was nearing completion, I didn't plan to remain in the Army. My goal was to return to the United States with my German wife. In the meantime, I was given the option to live off base and receive housing funds and separate rations. I moved with Krimhilde into an apartment, along with her sister and mother.

For some reason, Krimhilde never managed to complete the required paperwork to leave with me to the States. Believing she would do this, and certain of her love for me, I extended another seven months to spend a full three-year tour in Germany.

Since I thought we were leaving soon for the USA, I rejected an offer to reenlist for $10,000.

Finally, after finishing this extended tour, I returned to the States in 1972 to separate from the service, expecting Krimhilde to come. I moved back to Texas to reunite with my family.

Krimhilde was in no hurry to join me. My return to America became a long-suffered wait for my love, a love who would never come. A year passed. I spent $1000 on phone calls in a single month, an even more astronomical sum back then. I wrote Krimhilde a letter every day in German. She never wrote back.

Not willing to give up, I returned to Germany in 1973. Krimhilde again failed to do what was necessary for us to be together: registering her address so we could get married. It was yet another sign she wasn't serious about the relationship.

My arrival was quite a surprise to Krimhilde—and, it turned out, not a welcome one. During my time in the U.S., Rick Lovell, a Vietnam veteran and my best friend, confided to me that Krimhilde was stepping out and partying. I confronted her about it. Krimhilde denied it. Like countless others whose judgment was clouded by wishful thinking, I chose to deny the facts before me. I opted to trust her and believe what she said. As a result the pain and insult that culminated in our breakup would grow until it burst forth years later.

I registered to become a legal guest worker in Germany. I wooed Krimhilde relentlessly. Finally, two years later, after laying siege to the love of my life for more than three years, Krimhilde consented to marry. We wed on July 4, 1975, and moved into an apartment in Durlach, a suburb east of Karlsruhe. Karlsruhe would become my home for 30 years, and the home of longest duration I've ever had.

Right from the start, things went south. It was a tradition there that friends of the bride would kidnap her from the reception and that the groom was to seek them and pay the tabs of all the drinks wherever they were. I felt it more appropriate to stay with everyone at the reception and not be spending funds on such a frolic, as I saw it. This did not go well with Krimhilde or her brothers.

Also during the wedding celebration, we learned that my maternal grandmother had passed away. A shadow was cast over us from the start.

By the end of 1975, I was given the opportunity to transfer to the new Michelin tire plant in Greenville, South Carolina. It was a salaried position in production planning and quality control. I went expecting my wife to join me in three to six months. She never did. Indeed, Krimhilde never even applied for a visa.

Here, I must make clear my lack of innocence. While out with a friend back in America, I ran into his girlfriend and her friend. We drove them home. Once there we spend some time drinking and talking together. After my friend retired with his girlfriend to the bedroom, her friend made a pass at me. I did not reject it.

I ended up spending a lot of time with her and traveling with her to see the sights. She was an elementary-school teacher enjoying life, and was paying all of the expenses. I very much regret having had that sinful fling. Perhaps some of what I was to suffer was, if not divine punishment, to a certain degree not unjust.

In time, my position at Michelin USA changed. Krimhilde had made no progress in obtaining a visa, so I decided to return to Germany and rejoin my new bride. Back in Karlsruhe, I worked numerous jobs. I am something of a jack-of-all-trades and a quick study, as the Army learned during my time in the Finance Corps. A documented guest worker, I was given the opportunity to attend trade school. Two years later I was certified as a control-processing-instrumentation mechanic.

The carousing continued. In 1980 on a German holiday, Krimhilde went out dancing and did not return home until 5 a.m. This humiliation proved a spiritual experience for me. I felt deeply violated. I couldn't sleep even after she came home. Krimhilde got in bed, rolled over and went to sleep. From this time I began to be plagued by insomnia.

The humiliation reached its peak the next year. On August 31, 1981, nine months after this encounter, Krimhilde gave birth to a girl. She was noticeably darker than Krimhilde and I. Moreover, because a subsequent test confirmed my low sperm count, it was clear the child was not mine.

Krimhilde considered placing the child up for adoption. Ultimately she opted to keep her, after I encouraged her to do so and expressed my continuing commitment to the marriage. Only when she was a teenager of approximately 17 did I inadvertently mention that I was not her physical father. I assumed she knew. She did not. Krimhilde never told her.

I freely concede I was not squeaky clean in this situation because of my affair with the elementary-school teacher back in the States. Still, I wanted to make the marriage work.

I asked the familiar cry: "God, why me?" I wasn't angry. I felt deeply betrayed.

My itinerant jobs during this time required me to travel throughout Europe. This meant, as a practical matter, I would drive home for long stretches to see Krimhilde and our daughter—only to end up babysitting while she went out to the local clubs all weekend. When I became unemployed for a spell, this created even more stress and tension in the home.

I eventually took a job which required long stretches on the road. I spent weeks at a time away from home.

I would return to see a wife who didn't care to be married. I attended a wedding as a translator and joined the reception where Krimhilde was dressed very provocatively, dancing and cavorting with other men—our young daughter in tow. That memory sticks with me. I was devastated, demoralized, feeling lost and hopeless—castrated by events.

That night, I had an amazing experience I can only describe as spiritual. I believe, as he was leaving earth, my father's spirit gave me a final, short visit. Later that night we received a phone call from my family telling me that my father had passed away, and they had been trying to reach me for almost 24 hours.

I returned home for the funeral. One benefit was being able to spend time with my siblings, particularly my brother, from whom I had been estranged for some time. Don told me his war stories from Vietnam. That was difficult for him and for me. Don's first marriage had failed. Ironically, he met his second wife in Germany as I did—and remained with her until his death. Don and his wife settled near our hometown of Denison, Texas, on Lake Texoma.

I suffered chronic insomnia at this time due to Krimhilde's infidelity. When I was back in the States attending my father's funeral, I was unable to sleep. One night I walked outside to look around. I noticed, as I surveyed the darkened countryside, that when I turned my head, shadows would move. Strangely, it appeared light was emanating from me. I still believe the Holy Spirit visited me and illuminated me, resting as a flame on my head, and comforting me during this awful trial.

Upon my return to Germany, things got worse. Krimhilde would criticize everything I did: how I washed the dishes, not straightening up the sofa pillows after I got up, and so forth. I took to sleeping in my daughter's bed, not wanting to toss and turn and keep her awake. Krimhilde slept well.

In the late 1980s, the division between us became downright hostility, and persecution. When Krimhilde saw me praying in her daughter's room, she disparaged me. Through her actions, she encouraged her daughter to look down on me, as well. Krimhilde would laugh and yell as I prayed, saying, "Shut up!" I thought a demon was working through her, trying to silence me. I could not correct her because that would be dishonoring her in front of our daughter, but I could not allow her to dishonor me and my beliefs.

Unable even to practice my faith in my own home, I knew it was over.

I confronted Krimhilde one last time. I told Krimhilde, "You're living divorced. You're living in my place, using my money, being disrespectful, and not being any kind of wife."

She didn't really deny the charges. We were already effectively divorced. Soon, I took the legal steps to make it official.

Still, I couldn't let go. Even after we were divorced, I asked Krimhilde out to see a movie. She and I went out to see the film "The Bodyguard." Afterwards we went to a Christian café. As we sat there, my mind a mélange of love, confusion and sadness, Krimhilde asked, "What are your plans for life?"

I told her, "I don't know. I guess I want to do what the Lord wants me to do."

She then told me in German a phrase that I'll never forget: *"lass uns in ruhe!"* It was a German expression for "buzz off."

At this point, even someone who had ignored all the signs of rejection, to cling to a love that never existed, could take the hint, which was not subtle. Fourteen years after the birth of a child who wasn't mine, to a wife who never really wanted anything from me but money, I saw the writing on the wall. It was over.

Interestingly, Krimhilde never married again, nor, to my knowledge, had a serious relationship. She gave up on men after some more casual relationships. She later insisted we'd still be together if it weren't for me being such a religious fanatic.

My faith was not negotiable.

Here I should note that Krimhilde was born out of wedlock, as were her four siblings. Their father was an alcoholic. She was attracted to alcoholics throughout her life (our relationship was a decided exception). I believe infidelity and alcoholism were curses in her life that carried over into our relationship.

The Good Book poses the question: "Who can find a virtuous woman? For her price is far above rubies." (Proverbs 31:10). You won't find another man more in agreement with these principles.

I don't think Krimhilde ever loved me. It was all just a dream. As a result of the years of mistreatment and the dissolution of our marriage, my self-confidence and manhood were shredded. I had never played the field before. For all my faults, I had always wanted to have a solid marriage, and I was deeply wounded and unable to trust.

After we broke up, I was, like Jonah, in the whale's mouth. It was a testing period. I learned to wait and see how God wants to use me.

*   *   *

In time, it became clear God had other romantic plans for me.

In early 2003, I went on a German Christian dating website, *Feuer und Flamme* ("Fire and Flame"). I posted a profile. The website required a spiritual testimony of sorts. I shared how that I had traveled throughout Europe, and that I was a "Texan in Germany." I went on to explain that I enjoyed traveling and learning new languages.

I received about 10 to 15 contacts with diverse women. The most meaningful turned out to be Rose. We emailed and started texting each other, then began making phone calls.

Rose gives her recollection of how we met:

> After I saw a picture of Tom for the first time, I found it fits him very well. One day on the phone he was asking me if he could visit with me.
> And I said yes, why not.

Rose recognized my self-esteem was not what it once had been:

> And he didn't really expect anything and didn't understand what I was saying and answered, 'OK, maybe later.' It really took him a moment to realize that I said, 'Yes.' I told him that I would ask someone from

church that he could stay with him. Needless to say, he came right on the next day.

I recall it was a long holiday weekend in early May. I decided to drive the 500 miles north from South Germany to North Germany. Rose lived in Husum, on the Danish border and the North Sea, north of Hamburg. I drove up there in a new fitness training suit and arrived after approximately eight hours of driving.

Rose shared with me much later that it was as if I had a large L on my forehead—"L" for "loser." That's what I was projecting to her. I believe that's how I felt.

She invited me into her apartment. We departed shortly thereafter, walking to a nearby market square to share a meal in an Italian restaurant. Rose had arranged for me to sleep in an extra bedroom at the home of a single male member of her congregation, the Word of Life Church on the North Sea.

After spending the weekend there and attending church with her, I returned to Karlsruhe. With my self-confidence in the gutter, I assumed I'd never hear from her again. But she had seen some things she liked, and saw what was inside of me. She initiated an increase in communication. During many phone calls, we shared, from the inside out, our hearts, our desires, our hopes and dreams, our strengths and weaknesses.

I knew I'd found, at last, late in life, my soulmate. Rose sums up well what happened next, and very quickly:

> It was the weekend of July 3rd when I was visiting again, and that was the weekend when he first told me he loves me. And you would not guess but the next day July 4th he proposed!

We were married on October 10, 2003, in Husum.

Ironically, when Krimhilde met Rose, she liked her.

*　　　　*　　　　*

"Jesus wept." The shortest verse in the Bible is a reminder that we shouldn't fall into the trap of self-pity. Jesus didn't weep for Himself. He wept for the lost, and for others.

I devoted this chapter to love not to wallow in the misery of a lost love, and all that was lost along with it. Nor did I seek to tell merely the story of my true love, Rose—the wife of today whose face launches a thousand conversations in my car.

I speak of love, from my humble vantage point, because I think we've lost sight of what love really means. I see that every day in my car, with my passengers.

I think we should start by reminding ourselves of what God taught us about love. For God Himself is love. He expects us to understand the importance, meaning and relevance of love in our daily lives.

The most famous verse in the Bible is all about love:

"For God so loved the world, that he gave his only begotten Son, that whoever believes in him should not perish but have eternal life." (John 3:16)

The Bible also tells us:

"Dear friends, let us love one another, for love comes from God. Everyone who loves has been born of God and knows God." (1 John 4:7)

And:

"Whoever does not love does not know God, because God is love." (1 John 4:8)

We should approach God's love with awe and reverence, and know how love is supposed to govern our lives.

"If I have the gift of prophecy and can fathom all mysteries and all knowledge, and if I have a faith that can move mountains, but do not have love, I am nothing... And now these three remain: faith, hope and love. But the greatest of these is love." (1 Corinthians 13:2, 13)

"Above all, love each other deeply, because love covers over a multitude of sins." (1 Peter 4:8)

Love guides us and encourages us to be kind to one another: "Be completely humble and gentle; be patient, bearing with one another in love." (Ephesians 4:2)

And of course there is romantic love, the love that binds a man and a woman together. That's the kind I've been focusing on in my personal stories.

We are told, "There are three things that amaze me—no, four things that I don't understand: how an eagle glides through the sky, how a snake slithers on a rock, how a ship navigates the ocean, how a man loves a woman. (Proverbs 30:18-19).

The Bible gives other instruction:

"He who finds a wife finds what is good and receives favor from the Lord." (Proverbs 18:22)

Also, we're told that as a practical matter: "Two are better than one, because they have a good return for their labor: If either of them falls down, one can help the other up." (Ecclesiastes 4:9)

Reinforcing those values is the importance of fidelity:

"Therefore what God has joined together, let no one separate." (Mark 10:9)

"Let love and faithfulness never leave you; bind them around your neck, write them on the tablet of your heart. Then you will win favor and a good name in the sight of God and man." (Proverbs 3:3-4)

These teachings about love, and my experiences with love, both real and imagined, influence how I interact with my customers. The pain I have felt has seasoned and prepared me for those who are also hurting or looking for true love.

One Saturday night, I picked up Laura and took her on a ten-minute trip. She asked about Rose's picture. I affirmed she is my wife. She stated how beautiful she is and wanted to know how we met. One question led to another.

Seven minutes away from her destination, I was able to share a message from my life that clearly impacted her. I spoke of what the Lord has done in my life, and about some of my experiences. Laura said she was very encouraged and had hope.

Laura, you see, was about 40. She hasn't found the love of her life yet. My stories lifted her spirits so she gained renewed hope she would still find a soulmate.

I've focused on romantic love, but that of course is not the only kind. In other conversations and interactions, I strive to encourage a different kind of love—a fraternal, Christian love.

Sometimes I seek to show my love by stopping and picking up people who seem to need a ride. I offer a free ride when led by the Spirit. Of course, I can't do this for everyone. But when, for instance, I see an elderly or middle-aged person with his children walking along the road, or standing next to a car that's apparently broken down, I often stop and offer them a ride. It's not uncommon for this to turn into an opportunity to share an inspirational message.

Once, I picked up an Asian man who worked in a tattoo parlor in Cedar Springs. We drivers are encouraged to leave after five minutes if the passenger has not arrived. But he indicated through text messages he needed me to stay. I decided to wait. When he got in, I saw sitting in my back seat a humble elderly Asian man. He was very grateful and seemed touched that I would give up extra income to wait for him.

After he established he was from China, I spoke a bit of Chinese, as I often do. Again, I sought to let him know my love of him. He said "You're so kind," repeatedly. He expressed his gratitude and seemed genuinely touched that I had waited for him and tried to connect with him as a person during our short drive together.

If the conversation clarifies the passenger is from a certain country and I know some of the language, I use the words I know to help get the conversation going. They invariably appreciate it. I've found saying the word "namaste" to people from India carries a similar effect.

Having lived as an alien in Europe over half my life, I have a natural affinity for immigrants. Often I can speak some of their language. They are surprised and delighted by that. My travels have given me a little something for everyone. Some take exception to my using their language, but that is rare. One way I've sought to show love for others is to attempt to learn foreign languages. I believe this allows me to affirm others as worthy individuals, and humble myself so I don't come across as an arrogant American. I see looking back that my many years in Germany as an alien prepared me to have a heart for immigrants here in America.

The hurtful experiences I've shared here taught me how to recognize true love, and much more. I seek to encourage others who are hurting. I try to draw them out in our short time together in my car.

I encourage people by joking, as I drop them off at Love Field, one of the two major airports in the Dallas area: "I'm leaving you here under the banner of love."

My past has left its share of scars. Fear of rejection is a major problem for me. I am still not completely healed from the pains I've experienced. But I declare "It is healed in Jesus' name!" The temporal world may obscure the healing, as the deceiver pushes depression and darkness on us. But I can see the light and feel the healing power of Christ.

I show love by putting people on my prayer list. And I literally write some names on my palm, which remain there until the ink is washed away several days later. There is Abdul, the Turkish Muslim; Georgia, the prostitute who cursed me; Terry, the drunk who claimed to be a Christian; Brad, a young man I've met at church; and Lana, who is battling suicidal thoughts.

In that way I literally write the names of those needing my love on my hand, so I can't forget them.

Jesus took nails in His hands. I figure writing down some names on my palm, to help me remember to pray for them, is my own very small imitation of the love He showed us.

Chapter Four

Sin

"He waited to make sure we were at the right place."

I really like the above passenger review. For me it has a double meaning. So much of what Jesus taught us had a double meaning. His parables, for example, were rich with meaning on multiple levels.

The review above is one of my favorites because it has a double meaning to me. Yes, I do take pride in making sure my passengers arrive safely and are inside their intended destination before I leave. I don't earn quite as much money by staying and ensuring their safety. But it's the right thing to do.

I also like to leave my passengers in the "right place" mentally and spiritually. That means trying to guide them by the light of the Holy Spirit.

"Direct my footsteps according to your word; let no sin rule over me." (Psalm 119:133). May this be our motto in fighting sin.

Sometimes I get the sense that sin and darkness follows a passenger into my car. I've sensed that especially with those immersed in sexual perversions, such as prostitutes and active homosexuals. I ask God to use me, to affirm to these and other people they are unique individuals loved by God. I seek to influence them positively.

In the course of this work, I do get a sense of opposition. When Satan is angry, those under his control show that anger. They yell, rant and rave, curse.

I don't set myself up as a high-and-mighty judge of others. I've had the same battles with sin and temptation as all of my passengers. I just crawled to the foot of the cross to find a way to overcome. I must remind myself, "For all have sinned and fall short of the glory of God, and all are justified freely by his grace through the redemption that came from Christ Jesus." (Romans 3:23-24).

My life story says as much. I grew up just as blue laws were being repealed, and as the courts were legalizing pornography and allowing that and other related temptations to become commonplace. I remember as a teenager walking to school in Texas and finding a Playboy magazine on the side of the road. I consider pornography rocket fuel for sin. It was not a good encounter for me, nor has it been for many millions of men then and since.

Other times, I recall skipping out from Paris High School and going across the street to a place called Satan's. This was the local arcade, where they had pinball machines for 5 cents a game. I spent many lunch breaks there. When I won numerous games, I would often continue to play and skip school. This obviously wasn't a huge transgression, but the stage was set for larger ones down the road.

While in the Army and attending finance school in Indianapolis (Fort Benjamin Harrison), I found myself caught up in the snare of premarital sexuality that would become all too common for young men in later decades. On my first free weekend, I was enjoying the sights and sounds downtown when I met a sixteen-year-old girl named Brenda. We became romantically involved.

Unfortunately, my memory of one of the great achievements in human history is intermingled with my consciousness of sin. Brenda's parents were away from home and I was watching television with her. As Neil Armstrong took his famous first steps on the moon, she and I had intimate relations. I lost my virginity at a young age (shortly before my twenty-first birthday). I don't know, looking back, how this affected the course of my life—or hers, for that matter. Though a common sin, it was not a good start for a young life, then or now.

These and other experiences have made me sensitive to the hypersexuality and debauchery of our times. When I drive passengers to their favorite "watering holes" or obvious dens of temptation, I empathize. I do my best to steer them the right way when I can.

The weekend is the best time to minister. People are going out and returning from their false "good times." They are also more open to a message of hope and deliverance.

*   *   *

A few examples of passengers mired in sin give a sense of the moral pollution that has become so prevalent in our society at this time.

In May 2022, on a Saturday night, I picked up a white woman with brown hair, in her late thirties. She was wearing black-knit dress, a flared skirt that barely covered her private parts, and plenty of see-through mesh. Scantily clad was putting it mildly. She was leaving a hotel. I'll call her Georgia.

As I often do, I handed her one of my mock $1 million bills. The back of the bill carries an exhortation to follow Jesus. I told her, "A penny for your thoughts, a million for your heart." We began a conversation about the highest things possible.

This obvious prostitute said she had been raised in the Church of Christ. When she spoke of her beliefs, she offered a psychobabble about the "Fifth Dimension" and things I couldn't wrap my head around. I saw the opportunity to try to lead her back to the faith of her youth, before she had turned from the truth.

"Can I tell you what I believe?" I asked.

She didn't directly answer, and seemed to want to evade anything but giving her own view of things. Georgia capped off her secular sermon by saying, "We've all been lied to."

I did my best to point her towards the light. I did not give up easily. I wanted to tell her God allowed Jesus to be crucified for her. God wanted to burn away all the sin and unbelief that her adult years had built up on her.

But Satan resisted, and she would have none of it.

As I pulled up to another hotel, I could see the app saying, "Welcome, Mark." That must've been the name of her pimp, for that was certainly not her name.

As she left the vehicle, she laid into me.

"How dare you say my faith is wrong and yours is right!" Georgia screamed. She cursed at me. "You're making money off this trip"—as if I knew she was a prostitute when I accepted the trip assignment, or would've been in the right to reject her when I saw the way she was dressed.

Georgia stormed off by insisting, "I am going in to love these people!"

My final words were: "Jesus loves you. God loves you. God bless you."

As she left to meet her next client, I was left wondering if she would file a complaint with my company. Frankly, I didn't care. What I lack in station in life, I try to make up for in truth and courage.

I was at first overwhelmed with the natural feeling of failure. Because I had challenged her to reject a life of sin and selfishness and being exploited by other men, she had treated me with contempt. . I didn't allow the feeling of rejection to get the better of me. I drove on to my next divine appointment.

I've asked my wife Rose and another friend to join me in praying for Georgia.

The range of sin coming into my vehicle is in line with the sins of our times. I've picked up plenty of people I discerned to be prostitutes, both men and women. Sometimes I suspect passengers are couriers of drugs. The packages they carry suggest this, and I sense it in my spirit. Since I don't have the power or authority to challenge them, I pray silently.

Other times the scent of marijuana emanates from their clothing or persons. Someone once left a bottle of fentanyl in my car. Drugs are an ever-present vice and danger. Vaping is so common that I believe some partake of it in my back seat without asking permission.

To meet my passengers, I sometimes must walk into bars. Often I see provocatively clad women engaged in untoward behavior. Homosexual bars are also a common gathering place I occasionally must enter. Sports bars are big now, and the sports being conducted there on TV may be professional, but the local "sports" are often far from righteous.

Certain memories of passengers struggling with sin stick with me. One is a man who suffered from alcoholism. I picked him up from a bar in Dallas. He confided he had lost his girlfriend due to his drinking. Yet there he was, drinking still more. I was moved by his plight. I found there was little I could do besides safely drive him home.

Trips given to promiscuous homosexuals disturb me. On Halloween 2018, I picked up someone in the Cedar Springs area of Dallas. It is a notorious center of homosexual activities, with a large and vibrant LGBT nightlife. The public acts I saw—before Covid but during a rampant outbreak of Ebola—were troubling and memorable.

One experience that especially weighed on my soul involved a homosexual couple bragging of their exploits. Two young men—one Black, one white— entered my vehicle outside a hotel near Henderson Taphouse in Dallas. They commenced laughing and sharing how they'd just had a delightful time pleasuring one another, leaving behind oil residue and lubrication over all the hotel furniture.

Other times, I recall passengers who were obviously struggling with sin and didn't appreciate my gentle attempts to reach them spiritually. One male passenger named Terry, a white man about 40 years old, sat down in my back seat at around 1:30 a.m. He picked up the million-dollar bill I leave in the back seat.

He asked, "What's this?"

I replied, "It's a penny for your thoughts, a million for your heart."

Terry went on, asking me to relate what was on the bill. He complained the writing was too small for him to read it. I don't think that was the case, but I told him of the Christian message on the bill and did my best to share the gospel with him.

"This is trickery!" he exploded. "You're using trickery! You've got a captive audience and you're forcing people to read this!"

In fairness, Terry had been drinking and probably was not himself. He calmed down later, and even said he agreed with what I was saying. He just didn't like the tactic of "tricking" people. Despite his outburst and the profanity-laced commentary he offered, Terry insisted he was also a believer. He prayed "every night," he said.

We parted on good terms. I came away believing he was convicted, which was the whole purpose of the bill. For it is Satan who is the trickster. I believe he was speaking through Terry.

Are such people worth the effort. Of course! I've been called to minister to them with the time and opportunities that I have. I called it "loving the untouchables."

There is a connection between Jesus' crucifixion and God hugging us, stretching out His arms. For me it's like God saying, "Come to Papa! Let me squeeze the Devil out of you!" I try to love on these lost souls in the same way. Prostitutes, alcoholics, strippers and their patrons—none are lost for good. All can be reached with the gospel.

I firmly believe God has put me here, armed with faith and certain life experiences, to encourage them. I try to affirm people based on where they are in life, but in a proper direction. As the Bible says, I try to "restore that person gently." (Galatians 6:1)

I do this lovingly, as we are instructed to do. Jesus says in Matthew 18:15, "If your brother or sister sins, go and point out their fault, just between the two of you. If they listen to you, you have won them over."

That is my policy, or at least I try to follow it. But then there are those who will not listen. For them, you must draw a line.

Ephesians 5:11 teaches, "Have nothing to do with the fruitless deeds of darkness, but rather expose them." I try to follow this instruction faithfully.

Christian counseling is another way for God to speak to us. I believe counselors should enter into the throne room of God with people, ask challenging questions, and point people to Christ. This work must be done individually and in total submission to the Father's will. Likewise, there is nothing cowardly or wrong in seeking out counseling. I told a friend I've been ministering to that counseling is far better than hiding in one's home, afraid to go out and battle sin.

Everyone must find his own way. We must work out our salvation with fear and trembling. We don't hear this message very much anymore because it's a tough message. But it is right.

As someone who regularly drives immigrants from the Indian Subcontinent, I must note something else. We Christians in America and Europe can too easily look down on other cultures and peoples for their beliefs. Nations that practice polytheism are easy targets. But are we really so much better off?

The U.S. has millions of "gods," just like India, for example. That is to say, we worship material things that we want—and there are millions of them. We worship people we admire: entertainers, musicians, politicians, political parties, evangelists, comedians, charismatic people. We even worship our classic cars and Harley-Davidson motorcycles. Or we simply worship ourselves.

When we want something, too often we just rub God's belly and hope our desire pops out, like a genie in a lamp. Usually the belly they're really rubbing is their own.

Those who think they can live this way are wrong. We are told that explicitly, that these "wrongdoers will not inherit the kingdom of God." We are warned: "Do not be deceived: Neither the sexually immoral nor idolaters nor adulterers nor men who have sex with men nor thieves nor the greedy nor drunkards nor slanderers nor swindlers will inherit the kingdom of God." (1 Corinthians 6:9-10).

I've focused on the sins I see in my work, especially weekend runs. Much of this can be classified as partying, which involves sex, drugs and alcohol. Yet it is also sinful to crave the material things of the world, to crave its approval at the expense of doing the work of God.

I sense that sin clouds the lives of many people I pick up and drop off for work. Too often their work becomes their god. They seek to be admired for their possessions and bank accounts.

Yet we are told that "friendship with the world means enmity against God." And "anyone who chooses to be a friend of the world becomes an enemy of God." (James 4:4). Finally, "Do not love the world or anything in the world. If anyone loves the world, love for the Father is not in them." (1 John 2:15).

Many just don't believe or don't want to believe in Christ for the most self-centered and short-sighted of reasons. They fear it will affect their lifestyles, their relationships, even their jobs. This was true in the earliest days of the church. Nothing has changed except the names, places and jobs.

It's hard not to fall into the trap of keeping up with the rat race and seeking the world's approval. That too is a sin I see in my work. I do my best not to fall into that trap myself. "For the wages of sin is death, but the gift of God is eternal life in Christ Jesus our Lord." (Romans 6:23).

Sometimes, passengers share how sin has devastated their lives. On these occasions, there is little to be done besides listen and encourage.

Once I accepted a ride from Jamir, a Black man, after midnight. He arrived in a simple white T-shirt. I drove him to the milk plant where his brother worked to pick up his daughter's belongings. During our conversation, Jamir disclosed that his daughter had had sex with her cousin, the son of his brother.

I said, without condemnation, "We are living in perilous times." I offered encouragement and hope. I mentioned that's what the cross signifies.

When I dropped him off in Oak Cliff, a neighborhood in Dallas, we hugged each other. I believe I encouraged his spirit at a tough time. Perhaps some seeds were planted as well.

If nothing else, I want everyone to know, regardless of their past actions or characters, that all are welcome in my vehicle. The only one who's not welcome in my car is the devil. Sometimes he comes in with people, anyhow.

In time, through my conversations and actions, I make it clear they're welcome—but he's not.

Chapter Five

Hope

"I felt very positive while talking to him"

I know that every trip is a divine appointment. Our meetings are not accidents. They are literally a coincidence – co-incidents of people coming together according to God's plan.

These meetings bring opportunities. I've come to believe part of my mission is simple but important. It's to lift up people who are obviously down, searching. To give them, in a word, hope.

I feel the word "hope" should mean more than "I hope so." It shouldn't be tepid. Hope in the Biblical sense entails strong, energetic belief.

How do I try to bolster my passengers with hope? First, before I take the wheel, I try to wash away the cares and troubles of the day and drape myself with the mantle of hope. If you want to encourage others, you must find hope within yourself and lead by example. I try to do this daily. Seeing living examples of people living hopefully is, I think, the best possible inspiration.

In addition, I've found a couple of tactics helpful for raising people's spirits. One is music. You'd be amazed the difference music can make in lifting moods very quickly once in an automobile. Driving in the Dallas-Fort Worth metroplex is an adventure, as it is in most sprawling urban areas today. Road rage has become more of an obstacle to doing my job successfully.

But classical music has a calming effect on all. I began my affinity for classical music in my vehicle after I turned on a local classical-music station, WRR FM. I quickly became an avid fan. Afterwards, I purchased my first Beethoven CD.

Having lived in Germany over half my life, my appreciation for the German masters goes without saying. I followed up by buying several other CDs of classical music. I play them constantly. Passengers are very appreciative of the music and comment on it positively. Besides, much of modern music is full of celebrations of sin in various forms. That's not the message I want to share.

I sought to live by hope during the recent Covid troubles. During the two years of Covid lockdowns and precautions, I drove passengers without being vaccinated and without testing positive. Throughout this ordeal I have driven open Covid patients and Covid-positive dialysis patients, some of whom carried oxygen bottles with them. I hoped and trusted God would deliver me, despite my advanced age and constant exposure to risks. I worked to be like the Parabolani, the early Christians who ministered to the sick.

Throughout this time, as my rideshare efforts aided the afflicted, I believed God would protect me from harm and illness. And He did. I never tested positive, and am still going strong.

There is something else I leverage to try to instill hope in my passengers. It is my experience, shared with the many immigrants who use rideshare, at being an alien and an outsider. Being exposed to other lands and hearing other languages have given me the experience of being an alien each time I cross the ocean, flying between Texas and Germany. I have empathy for the many foreigners who take rides with me.

For a good example, I'll share with you a sampling of passengers I drove during Memorial Day weekend of 2022. It was, shall we say, an international weekend for me. In quick succession I met people from across the globe and was able to share hope and good news with them.

I met a Turkish man who picked up the million-dollar bill. Mohammed realized from my rideshare profile I had lived in Germany. He asked me if I knew any Turks. I responded that I had, and talked about them. I also mentioned my admiration for Mustafa "Ataturk" Kemal, the great Turkish leader who modernized Turkey. I shared with him that my friend Dorca, a Christian missionary, serves in Turkey. I had every impression he left my vehicle with hope, joy and a feeling of acceptance in a country where he was still new.

Another Turk hailed a ride from me. A young man, he spoke excellent English. He plied me with many questions about my background and travels. Eventually, I was able to share the gospel message with him. He was very receptive and left my presence knowing my good intentions.

Missionaries often exude hope. I picked up one, Julia, who stands out. A young African woman, Julia hailed a ride in the early evening outside The Upper Room, a vibrant church east of downtown Dallas in the old commercial area. I drove her about thirty minutes, driving her west to DFW, the main airport. Julia shared she was from Africa and was just passing through Dallas, on her way to a mission in Mexico. I was able to pray for her and encourage her. She expressed her gratitude. We gave our Heavenly Father all the glory.

Another African, Benedict from Nigeria, entered my vehicle that weekend. I drove him down to Commerce Street in Dallas. Around thirty years old, Benedict took my million and looked at it. I gave my standard ice-breaking line: "A penny for your thoughts and a million for your heart." It was a relatively short drive, but I shared with him when I could and seemed to plant some hopeful seeds.

I had a lovely conversation that same weekend with Kavika, originally from south India. She loved the million and we struck up a conversation. She confided her father had passed away and it still weighed on her, as she was still grieving. Kavika, like many, was curious about my world travels, and I gave some of my better stories. She had come to Texas by way of Oregon, she said. I drove her out to Krugerville, almost an hour away. I could see from her radiant face that the conversation had encouraged both of us.

Of course, not every conversation goes so hopefully. Sometimes one must deal with a great amount of pain just below the surface.

I picked up Cara right behind the Waffle House in North Plano. I drove her to her home in Rowlett. The million got the ball rolling.

"A penny for your thoughts, a million for your heart," I said.

I had no idea the door I was opening. Cara had just left a treatment center. She told me she had attempted suicide eight times. This was because of pain that she's unable to deal with, and that no medical professional can properly diagnose and treat.

I encouraged her to seek peace in Jesus. "Don't let the devil stop you from worshipping God and giving Him praise," I said. "Worshipping God and thanking Him for healing, in spite of whether we see manifest or not, strengthens our souls. Our healing has been purchased at such a high price on the cross."

Cara was a battered soul, in body and mind. She was overweight, and legs bandaged up. I couldn't tell if the wounds were self-inflicted.

I've found thoughts of suicide come from a deep unhappiness with life. There's a certain amount of self-hate at work. The enemy encourages those thoughts.

For almost half an hour after I drove her home, Cara stayed in my car talking with me. I turned off my app. We talked at length, and I shared as much encouragement as I could. Later, I texted her with a link to a local Christian event notice for prayer and fasting. I've added her to my prayer list.

I was tempted to look her up and follow up with her, given her grave situation. But company policy won't allow it, and I don't want to be too pushy in such a delicate situation. Instead, I commend her to the hands of the Almighty God, to whom all of us must ultimately hand over those we care about.

I can't end my discussion of hope amidst recent immigrants without sharing about Ranil, who is from India. Ranil's salvation came out of riding with me. I befriended him. In time I learned he was having trouble battling alcohol. I took Ranil out to eat at my expense. Then I took him to church. Our fellowship together bore good fruit.

Today, Ranil is saved! His mother was deeply grateful to me for helping guide Ranil onto a better path. Our time together doing simple things, such as sharing tea and coffee and praying together, helped fortify his experience with Christ. Today, he and his mother are personal assistants/servants for a well-to-do elderly couple in Austin, Texas. There they share the gospel message of love and servitude through their actions as well as their words.

*   *   *

The Lord gives messages of hope, of course, in the Bible. Here are some of my favorites:

"For I know the plans I have for you, declares the Lord, plans for welfare and not for evil, to give you a hope and a future." (Jeremiah 29:11)

"And now, O Lord, for what do I wait? My hope is in you." (Psalm 39:7)

"Surely there is a future, and your hope will not be cut off." (Proverbs 23:18)

"He is not afraid of bad news; his heart is firm, trusting in the Lord." (Psalm 112:7)

"May the God of hope fill you with all joy and peace in believing, so that by the power of the Holy Spirit you may abound in hope." (Romans 15:13)

Messages of hope can be found in the most straightforward of encounters. I once picked up

Kevin in downtown Dallas after work. He had a long trip home, up north to near Frisco, an affluent suburb. He was in his thirties, with red hair worthy of his Irish-blessed name.

Kevin mentioned he had gone through what he saw as a spiritual experience, an awakening of sorts. A "higher being" made it clear he was being taken care of, out of the chaos in his life. As I saw the doors open from Kevin's comments, I gently shared some biblical truths. I mentioned my own experiences with Jesus Christ. We both left grateful for the conversation and time together.

Madeline was a teacher who took a ride with me. She enjoyed the million and we began conversing. We talked about Covid, the school lockdowns and the effects on young people. Our conversation was more cultural than spiritual. Yet I believe some light entered her life through the interaction, and she left joyful.

Sometimes, hope can be injected just by taking a little extra time. One early evening I picked up Denny, a young man in Oak Cliff. He had just left a tumultuous living situation behind and was pleased to moving to Denton, a Dallas suburb, to be a father to his child. The place taking him in was Christian.

He began speaking about his excitement and sharing some of his recent troubles with me. A door opened. I shared the love God wanted to pour out to him. In turn, Denny spoke excitedly of all God was doing in his life. The trip went for around an hour.

It was pouring rain when I arrived at his new home. I stopped my meter and helped him unload his belongings. Then, just before leaving, I embraced him, somewhat awkwardly, to remind him of the hug of the Father—to squeeze the devil and sin and selfishness out of us. Denny was moved and hugged me back.

A couple more recent stories from 2022 help to capture my views and experiences related to hope. When I picked up Colin near Southern Methodist University, it came out that he too was a Christian. He was extremely grateful to run into another believer who was unabashed in sharing his testimony. Of course, the million was well received also.

Finally, a personal story shows the power of hope. Going back and forth between America and Europe has created a challenge for my lodging. In 2022 I returned from Germany without a lease. I wasn't sure what I would do. Rents had soared and my need for short-term housing made things difficult. I turned to the only solution that has always worked for me. I prayed.

I felt God told me he would provide the quarters I needed, but I should thank Him beforehand to show my faith. I did so, saying repeatedly "thank you" to the Most High God. Within an hour a woman named Maria called. A missionary sister with Christ for the Nations Institute, she said she was in the Dominican Republic and heard I needed a room. She offered me her room for the time being. Later I received another offer for a reasonably priced room. These were blessings I needed in a pinch and that God delivered after merely asking me to thank Him ahead of time for the coming blessing.

Such blessings, given out of the blue and at a time of great need, are, for me, a source of tremendous hope and inspiration. They remind us that the author of hope is capable of anything.

Chapter Six

Joy

"My night was made by our conversation"

People young and old are often surprised by my age. When I tell them I'm 74 (I've been alive almost three-fourths of a century!), they are curious. The most common question: What is the secret for looking young?

I am not sure how young I look, but give most of the credit to my beautiful young wife Rose. Yet I do think there's a certain vibrancy to the life I lead. It comes from doing what I enjoy: loving God and loving people.

My passengers learn quickly of my travels and time in Europe. The stories I tell reveal a life torn between two continents, a tension forged by my loves in Germany. Stories of foreign lands always interest us because they bring us information about things we don't know firsthand. In my case, my travels bring me joy.

I believe God has called all of us to be diamonds. Diamonds, of course, are formed through extreme pressure and heat. And when they come into being, they are both light giving and light receiving. All colors of the rainbow are present. That's how I try to share my gift—joyful illumination.

Let us consider what the Bible says of joy.

"Nehemiah said, 'Go and enjoy choice food and sweet drinks, and send some to those who have nothing prepared. This day is holy to our Lord. Do not grieve, for the joy of the Lord is your strength.'" (Nehemiah 8:10)

"You will go out in joy and be led forth in peace; the mountains and hills will burst into song before you, and all the trees of the field will clap their hands." (Isaiah 55:12)

"For his anger lasts only a moment, but his favor lasts a lifetime; weeping may stay for the night, but rejoicing comes in the morning." (Psalm 30:5)

"My lips will shout for joy when I sing praise to you— I whom you have delivered." (Psalm 71:23)

"I have told you this so that my joy may be in you and that your joy may be complete." (John 15:11)

And sometimes joy comes from difficult circumstances: "Consider it pure joy, my brothers and sisters, whenever you face trials of many kinds." (James 1:2)

Joy can be seen in a variety of ways. One night I took from Allen to the airport a Black woman in her thirties, with braided hair. She was to fly to visit her mother. I received what I'd call a "faith-complicit reaction."

It began when I commended her for honoring her parents, as the Ten Commandments requires. She praised and thanked God that we were having a divine appointment. I ended by calling her sister. We spend time talking about Scripture and the church being the bride of Christ.

I dropped off Karen at an elder housing community in Plano. I gave her joy by helping her unload her groceries.

Sometimes I gaze upon the buildings being constructed as such as furious pace around the Dallas area. There are of course many houses being erected. Some are small, some are sprawling mansions. Huge stores, office buildings and warehouses fill out the landscape. I think about the dreams and hopes of people who built or began to build houses only to see everything wither away. Yet joy comes from building, and hoping, and dreaming. These buildings symbolize that.

I think also of the different peoples that have lived here. The Plains Indians, the Spanish, the French, the Mexicans, the Texans, and now the Americans. What brought all of them joy? For many it was the promise of eternal life in Christ Jesus.

*   *   *

Ironically, I think we best find joy by walking humbly, and seeking out happiness in less lofty places.

Many prefer a "higher than thou" attitude. They think we need to be set apart to be great and happy with our lives. This is a lie of Satan.

We should not seek recognition. Christ forbade his followers from telling others of his miracles, knowing, of course, they would disobey and tell of these wonders anyhow.

Sometimes pride makes us see things as bigger than they are. Mere petty struggles with the flesh can seem overwhelming. We magnify these daily battles into spiritual battles of greater significance than our need to humbly and daily strengthen the spirit.

I believe we must live as Christ taught us to live: humbly. We must beware of pride. It comes before the fall, and I've seen so many people fall.

Meeting each other on the same plane, on the same page, as equals before God is, to me, the key to humility.

I believe this approach helps me to relate better to people. I focus on letting the Holy Spirit connect passengers to me. I try to communicate the love of God to people, affirming them as unique individuals, and let His light shine on them. Their lives may be broken, but that broken pottery is beautiful in God's eyes, and He will fix it.

Our pride has to shrink. Cain killed Abel out of pride. God will lift us up, not our own pride or efforts. When we rely try to lift ourselves up without leaning on God, that is pride working and it is unreliable in the long run. Pride can easily knock us right back down where we started.

During spiritual warfare I have found that worshipping and praising Jesus will force the demons and evil thoughts attacking us to withdraw. The joy of the Lord is our strength. The truth will set us free, and He is the truth. If we are indeed born again, we are safe in Him. He is our salvation, healer and Lord. Having paid off all our debts through His passion, bearing all of our sins through His suffering unto death through the torture of crucifixion, Christ has done His holy work. God also has sent unto us His Holy Spirit. It is the Holy Spirit that dwells in us, as well as comforts, guides, directs and protects us.

When we raise up our Lord in our hearts, His Spirit rises up within us, lifting our spirits to embrace Him: truth, victory and freedom. When we are weak He is strong. We must take Jesus at His word when He proclaims, "It is finished." When we trust and obey Him, motivated by His love for us, selflessly loving everyone else and hating no one but Satan and evil, we will find our peace and our salvation.

On those days when I grieve over things lost, or feel the pain and sting of the hurts of the past, I must remind myself: Out of bitterness can grow the greatest joy. For that joy is fertilized with profound tears.

How else do I gain joy? I admit I take satisfaction in seeing how well my passengers think of me, a simple old man who drives them places and shares the gospel as he can.

The reviews and comments people leave are little sprigs of joy for me. I share with you a few more that I haven't listed in chapter epigraphs before.

I confess they bring me joy:

"Thank you for the educational talk...God bless you"

"Such a sweet man"

"world-class gentleman"

"best ride I ever had"

"best driver ever"

"Thanks, Thomas. God bless you."

I am getting a big head here. So I'd better end. I don't want to start wearing a Texas-size "ten gallon hat"!

Joyful tears come to eyes as see the difference I made with people Jesus died for. Even the ones who were more difficult, who required more patience—even they and the memories of our time together bring me joy.

Chapter Seven

The King's Highway

"Thomas rocks!"

When I need to be reminded of how blessed I am, and why, I think of Dietrich Bonhoeffer.

A Lutheran pastor and theologian in Germany, Bonhoeffer traveled between his native country and the United States, much as I do. In his day, though, the stakes were much higher. He lived during the Nazi regime. And unlike so many in his era, he could not quietly put up with their atrocities.

It is easy, of course, to criticize affairs in another country from abroad, where one is safe. But Bonhoeffer chose not to do that. He returned from the safety of the United States to Germany. He spoke out against Hitler's policies. He criticized in particular the regime's euthanasia program and genocide against Jews. He worked with those who felt compelled to have Hitler assassinated.

Eventually, the Gestapo learned of his activities and arrested him. He was incarcerated at a prison camp. Along with others who supported efforts to remove

127

Hitler from power, Bonhoeffer was tried and convicted. In April 1945, just days before U.S. forces liberated his prison yard, Bonhoeffer was hanged. His final words were stirring: "This is the end—for me, the beginning of life."

I draw inspiration from his life because both of us straddled the Atlantic and shared the Christian faith. But his heroism is a model for all ages.

Today, the courage required of us is different but just as pressing. As in his day, the need for a Christian morality remains strong. While we don't suffer death for our Christian beliefs in the West, we suffer financially, professionally, socially. There is still a great deficit of Christian bravery and valor.

Like Bonhoeffer, I've walked the streets of Europe and see its decay. I see that same decay here. From my little outpost, my rideshare car, I do what I can to push back.

I take calls from friends and people I am supporting, to encourage them along. I helped lead Jacob and Ranil to the Lord. I've known Jacob for seven years. He's made great advances. I encourage him as he speaks of the spiritual warfare he perceives around him, attacking him with confusion and accusation.

In my dealings with anonymous passengers and those I've befriended in the service of Christ, I try to relate everything back on a personal level to what I've learned. This book is an attempt to do that for you, the reader. The ordinary experiences, the daily work for those needing a ride, the heartache and shattered relationships I've experienced—in all of these accounts I've been honest, and sought to help others. I do the same in my car as I go about my work.

I'll admit I see Christian leaders, groups and movements around me that I think are falling short of what is needed. We need courage today, not goody-goody, phony positive preaching. Yes, we must encourage. But we must also be honest. We must avoid vain religion at all costs.

Here I find myself drawn to this passage from James (Jacob) 1:26-27: "If someone believes they have a relationship with God but fails to guard his words then his heart is drifting away and his religion is shallow and empty. True spirituality that is pure in the eyes of our Father God is to make a difference in the lives of the orphans, and widows in their troubles, and to refuse to be corrupted by the world's values." (TPT)

I believe true religion is found only in the shadow of the Father, doing what we see the Father doing—as Christ Jesus taught us. This is a childlike relationship of trust. Constantly I am reminded of that old song: "We can only be happy in Jesus if we trust and obey, for there is no other way!"

Sometimes I feel ministers and others try to snuff out good and righteous fires in the faithful, probably without realizing it. We feed our head with facts apart from spiritual growth. Our pride is inflamed at the urging of those who say we can seek wealth even as we serve a Savior who said we should shun it.

Too many denominations, in my judgment, operate as cults. Their motto seems to be, "Our way is the only way." God has allowed many Christian churches to be born and to multiply on this earth. While He desires unity in service of Him, I can't believe He rejoices in denominations warring against one another. Christ the Peacemaker must be at the center of all we do.

When we are born again, we are "raptured into" to the heavenlies. We are transported to the heavenly realm into the Father's presence, standing on holy ground, cleansed inside and out by Christ's blood. Paul, for example, had what I believe was a "pre-trib rapture." This is the goal I have for new Christians: to seek this place of peace and joy.

Another quibble: I don't believe in idolizing analysis. I pronounce "analyze" as Anna Lisa. That can become an affair of sorts. Faith is to be taken as face value, as a child takes it. Those who dress it up as more than Jesus intended, I believe, do an injustice.

How do we, as a society, grow closer to God? Here are a few things I've seen along the way.

Popular entertainment has become a millstone around many necks. It's become a pagan babysitter and a source of much darkness. Television, films, social media—all can encourage self-isolation and unbelief. We are bombarded constantly with information and much of it inflames selfishness and sin.

I am old enough to remember the goodness that comes from simple peace and quiet. Peace does come with that quiet. I am a firm believer we should carve out that time daily for reflection, prayer, and just mental rest.

The effects of this social conditioning are obvious. People living in their own personal virtual reality often ignore and avoid anything that rocks their boat. Few find the courage to stand alone. Most are willing to defer to those who say they'll make decisions for them, if only they give them their vote and their lifestyle.

By the same token, people too often use religion to try to gain obedience and good behavior from their children. Yet they won't follow the faith themselves. We forget, as was recognized in earlier times, obedience is the key to serving God.

Another thing: I think we need to replace the word "believe" with trust. Trusting is what gets us to obey. Trust and obey—two great words you don't hear together much anymore.

When I look at Christ and trust in Him, I am healed. Belief manifests the healing, whether we see it now or later.

I've found prayer and fasting lead us closer to God. They do not necessarily move Him to do what we wish. It can, however. Our actions count.

It grieves me to see the spread of socialism here, which in many ways is a rejection of these eternal truths. I saw firsthand the devastation this ideology caused in Europe, especially East Germany. There, staples such as food were cheap, but high-quality goods were very expensive—because they were rare. Such is communism. Social responsibility is indeed a Christian value. Yet we need to find the right balance, rewarding productivity but not neglecting our fellowman.

Young people in America are being taught the wrong view of freedom. I know because I, like refugees of Marxist and socialist nations, have seen the awful fruit of those destructive ideologies.

There is also a vast misunderstanding of love. People talk about love in a way that kills true love. God gave us and showed us true love. He hates sin because it destroys people. Yet love lifts us up. If not motivated by God's unconditional love, we are lost.

My view of fundamental love is simple: Love is Christ ripped and crucified in my place.

Christ drank from two cups: the cup sharing with his disciples at the Last Supper, and the one of God's wrath, which was the torture he endured during his Passion. We tend to focus on His love and not the cup of God's wrath. We do well to take account of both. After all, He's paid for both.

I end by quoting a German word that works well today. Many suffer from a calloused heart. In German the word for callous sounds like that. It is *hornhaut*, which means literally "horned skin." We are told that things will get rough in the end times. Whether these are those times, only God knows for sure. But let us not allow our hearts to be so calloused that we can't find and show true love to one another.

Those are some of the principles I follow in my rideshare work. They are not fancy, or original, or brilliant. But I believe they are true, because Christ teaches them.

Some things, I'll admit, are above my spiritual pay grade. I ended my time in the Army as a specialist (Spec 5) or equivalent to a sergeant in grade. I call myself now an NCO (noncommissioned officer) in the Army of the Lord.

I don't drive a tank for Him. A simple car seems to suffice.

I'll keep rolling and sharing and loving as long as our Maker deems fit to give me that opportunity. And I'll never stop sharing the only message that really matters.

Acknowledgments

This book is filled with stories from many passengers who have blessed me with their time and conversations. I am deeply grateful and honored to have earned their trust and attention during my drives with them.

I am grateful to my beautiful German/Romanian bride, Rose Beshears (my "Gypsy Woman"), who has been a rock of faith, love and hope for me. Rose has been a great match for me in many ways. My American Indian blood is in line with the Gypsy blood in hers. She has encouraged me to rise up and flourish as a man of God.

I thank my parents, Herman and Martha (Parsons) Beshears, for the gift of life and for raising me to the best of their ability.

Thanks to Envoy America for a wonderful professional rideshare experience.

I also wish to thank pastors and others who have helped to guide me spiritually over the years: Pastor Raymond England, Trinity Lighthouse Church, Denison, Texas; the faculty and staff at Christ for the Nations Institute, Dallas, Texas; Adam McCain, Dean of Students and Pastor, The Hill Church, Cedar Hill, Texas (formerly Church on the Hill); Pastor Dr. Edward Calderon, Word International Church, Plano, Texas; Eitz Chaimn, Messianic Congregation, Plano, Texas; Rabbi David Schiller; and Pastor Ryan Binkley, Create Church, Richardson, Texas. I would also like to thank Walter Buehl, who has faithfully supported our ministry work in Europe, the U.S. and Mexico.

Thanks to the Original Pancake House of Plano, Texas, where I enjoy Christian fellowship regularly and great meals.

Thanks to my scribe, Andy Thomas, for helping me write this book.

Above all, thanks to God Almighty, for giving us cars, and people to talk to, and a gospel to share. To Him be all the glory.

... Jesus said to them, "With people this is impossible, but with God all things are possible."

Matthew 19:26 NASB 1995

138

About the Author

Thomas L. Beshears is a Vietnam-era non-combat veteran of the U.S. Army, a laborer in many fertile fields in Europe and America, and a born-again, Spirit-filled Christian who loves the Lord and the gospel we are called to share. He is currently a rideshare driver for a large rideshare company as well as a driver for a medical transport company. Tom currently lives in Texas in the Dallas-Fort Worth Metroplex, where he earns his living.

E-Mail: TomRIDESHARECOWBOY@gmail.com

kornerstonemedien@gmail.com

Made in the USA
Middletown, DE
31 October 2023